Sex, Meaning and the Menopause

Other books by Sue Brayne

The D-Word: Talking about Dying

Sex, Meaning and the Menopause

SUE BRAYNE

continuum

Published by the Continuum International Publishing Group

The Tower Building   80 Maiden Lane
11 York Road   Suite 704
London   New York
SE1 7NX   NY 10038

www.continuumbooks.com

First published 2011

British Library Cataloguing-in-Publication Data
A catalogue record for this book is available from the British Library.

ISBN: 978-0-8264-2301-6

Typeset by Pindar NZ, Auckland, New Zealand
Printed and bound in India

From the Red to the Silver

Between the red and the silver,
life unfolds in a dream.
Every step is a new step,
because I no longer bleed.

Moving from the red to the silver,
I only know what I'm told.
I once knew what my body feels,
but now it's an unknown world.

Changing body, changing mind,
this land is unexplored.
What defines me as woman now?
Not fertile, yet not old.

Caroline Born ©2009

Contents

Acknowledgements   xiii

A younger woman's understanding of the menopause   xix

Introduction   1
    What this book offers   4
    So, what *is* the book about?   5
    Structure   6
    A word about the male menopause   7

1   Myth-making: menopause and society   9
    The focus on sex   11
    Menopause: a medical diagnosis   12
    Drugs for sex   12
    The anti-ageing lobby   16
    Cultural differences   17
    A Second Menopause? God forbid!   20

2   Myth-busting: real, lived experiences   21
    Fading beauty   24
    Mothers and daughters   27
    Some find it a relief   28
    Easier transition for some   29
    End of fertility   30
    The sandwich generation   31
    Older single mum   32
    Living alone   33
    Much happier alone   34
    Credibility in the workplace   36
    Hitting their stride   39
    Ageing in the sex industry   40

3   **Menopausal mechanics of sex**   43

   Talking about sex   43
   The taboo of sex and the menopause   44
   Mechanical changes in sex   48
       1   A surge in sexual feelings   48
       2   Still enjoying sex   49
       3   Losing interest   51
       4   'Sudden death'   55
       5   Horribly painful   58
       6   Relieved it's all over   61
   Gay relationships   63
   The need for good communication   64
   Sexual differences   67
   Male masturbation and sex toys   68
   Female masturbation and sex toys   69
   Pornography   70
   Affairs   72
   Divorce   74
   Prostitution   75
   Menopause power!   76
   SWOFTIES abroad   77

4   **Meaning and the menopause**   79

   The inner call   80
   Midlife: a psychological crisis   81
   Midlife: a spiritual process   82
   Menopause: the struggle   83
   Menopause: a sacred state   85
   Love and self-healing   86
   The process of liberation   87
   Sex and spirituality   91
   Sex and sin   91
   Going beyond sex   94
   Using ritual   95
   Wisdom from the silver-haired   98

5   **Men talking about the menopause**   103

   Ray, 62 – The word I use is despair   104
   Brian, 53 – We've always had an open relationship   106
   David, 59 – Menopause highlights the cracks already there   108

Chris, 52 – The media are hopeless when it comes to the
menopause 111
Nick, 53 – There's nothing wrong with porn, if that's all there
is on offer 113
Will, 59 – Sex isn't just about penetration 115
Gary, 67 – I suppose it was the male menopause 117
John, 51 – It's not about sex, it's about pulling together 120
Daniel, 66 – Different planets is an understatement 123

6 Managing the menopause 127
   Talking to doctors 127
   Sensible resources 128
   Getting the best from your GP 130
   The HRT conundrum 132
   Basic facts about HRT 132
   HRT and sex: a short recap 133
   Women talking about HRT 135
   Coming off HRT 137
   Localized HRT 139
   Things to be aware of if you want to take HRT 140
   Natural alternatives 140
   Natural lubricants 144
   Dealing with hot flushes 145
   Sleeping separately 146
   Seeking emotional support 147
   Basic listening skills 147
   Keeping fit 149
   Exercise can help stress incontinence 150
   Yoga 150
   Dancing 152

Message to Meg 155

Recommended reading 159

Helpful websites 163

Index 165

Menopause is a liminal state, which means it's dangerous. But what's on the other side of the divide is unbelievable. I know that for sure because I've crossed the divide. So I know right now for the planet it's hot flushes and cold wars, depressive states, all this stuff. Also a lot of new ideas, a lot of chaos, and this emotional roller coaster and intellectual confusion. This babble of voices. All of what is part of this tremendous process.

Paula Gunn Allen in *Red Moon Passage* by Bonnie J. Horrigan

Dedicated to:

All you men who are struggling to make sense of what your womenfolk are experiencing.

Acknowledgements

First and foremost, thank you Andrew Walby for fighting my corner with your bosses at Continuum. This book couldn't have happened without you. Thanks also to Robin Baird-Smith for your support and encouragement, and to everyone at Continuum who helped to bring this book to life.

I am most grateful to Professor Julie Winterich, Professor Lorraine Dennerstein, Professor Adele Green and Professor Rob Pope. Sincere appreciation also goes to Dr Adrian Clarke, Wendy Maltz, Liz Copestake, Sue Friston, Alexandra Pope, Kathryn Colas, Norma Goldman, Hananja Brice-Ystma, Wendy Buonaventura, Hazel Kayes, Linda Parkinson-Hardman, Christine Webber, Caroline Born, and Virginia Ironside.

Love and gratitude to Maggie Cooper, my spiritual director at St Bueno's. Many thanks also to the awesome Helen Hammond from Elephant Creative Solutions. To Judi and Tig, my yoga gurus, and to Mike and Simone for all those death by aerobics classes! And to Janice, my Pilates and tap-dancing teacher. One of the liveliest and most inspiring postmenopausal women I know.

Special, special thanks to all the women and men I interviewed. Your honesty, integrity and courage was breathtaking, and when I started to wilt with the momentous task of writing this book, thinking of you all gave me the impetus to carry on. I hope I have done you justice.

Finally, heartfelt appreciation and love go to my husband Mark. He was with me every word of the way, and was, and continues to be, a constant source of inspiration, love and support.

Basic facts about the menopause

What does the word menopause mean?
The word *menopause* originates from the Greek, *pausis* (cessation).

Literal meaning: *meno* (month) pause (ceasing): A woman's last period.

Clinically, a woman is postmenopausal when she hasn't had bleeding or spotting for twelve months.

Average age in UK for natural menopause
Fifty-one years.

Stages of the menopause
Perimenopause: Hormone levels begin to change and fall.
Phase can last for up to ten years before the final period.
Signs include irregular periods or excessive bleeding.

Menopause: Hormone levels drop and menstruation ceases causing:
- **physical symptoms**, such as hot flushes, headaches, hair thinning, weight gain, memory loss, loss of sexual desire;
- **psychological symptoms**, such as mood swings, depression, anxiety attacks, general dissatisfaction with life (although psychological factors may well have been experienced long before the menopause) or feelings of liberation.

Postmenopause: The completion of the menopause (no bleeding or spotting for 12 months). Biologically a woman is no longer ovulating or menstruating and is incapable of conceiving a child.

Premature menopause
Affects around 1 per cent of women under the age of 40, and approximately 0.1 per cent under 30.

Menopause can happen in three ways
1 *Naturally* as ovaries cease to produce hormones.
2 *Surgically* (removal of uterus and/or ovaries: partial or total hysterectomy).

Most common cause is fibroids. Most common age for a hysterectomy is between 35 and 55.

3 *Chemically* (for example, in the treatment of cancer: radiotherapy, chemotherapy and hormone-repressing drugs).

Main hormones affecting menopause

- Oestrogen
- Progesterone
- Androgens (includes hormones such as testosterone).

What happens during the menopause?

Menopause is triggered by the shutting down or removal of the ovaries. The ovaries are part of the endocrine system which produces hormones. Sex hormones (predominantly progesterone and oestrogen) produced in the ovaries fall to extremely low levels, which means that eggs are no longer produced and fertility ceases. This fall in hormones affects every aspect of a woman's body, from sex drive to brain function.

How long do symptoms last?

The menopause is a very individual experience. Some women have few symptoms, while others can still be experiencing symptoms years after menstruation has ceased.

Some statistics

One-third of the female population in Western societies is currently going through the menopause.

By 2025, the World Health Organization estimates that 1.1 billion women worldwide will have reached the menopause. Approximately 25 million women each year will reach the menopause after that.

Approximately 8 out of 10 women in the UK experience symptoms leading up to the menopause. Around 45 per cent find their symptoms difficult to deal with.

Approximately one third of women lose interest in sex during perimenopause.

Around 40 per cent lose interest in sex during menopause.

Hormones which affect the menopause

PROGESTERONE: Levels drop during perimenopause

Source of progesterone
Mainly in the ovaries.

Role of progesterone (geared towards helping fertility)
- Generates production of blood vessels
- Helps to stabilize blood sugars
- Involved in fat metabolism and diuretics (removal of water from body)
- Elevation of mood
- Prevention of tumours
- Balances hormones to reduce anxiety
- Stimulates ovulation each month
- Orchestrates other hormones at ovulation to prepare uterus to receive fertilized egg
- Helps sperm to reach egg so fertilization can take place
- Stops after last period.

Progesterone diminishes during perimenopause causing symptoms such as
- Excessive blood clots/no bleeding/irregular bleeding
- Sore and/or swollen breasts
- Water retention
- Zinc deficiency (can cause depression or oversensitivity).

OESTROGEN
Source of oestrogen
1 Mainly from ovaries (made up from three hormones oestrone, oestradiol and oestriol).
2 Conversion from androgens found in other parts of the body to the hormone oestrone.

Affects all parts of the body including:
- Nerve cells
- Blood cells to brain.

Role of oestrogen

- Regulates menstrual cycle and pregnancy
- Prevents formation of free radical toxins
- Feeds blood vessels to skin
- Lubricates vagina and vulva
- Helps to protect bone density.

Production of oestrogen is directly affected by

- Body weight extremes, i.e. obesity or anorexia
- Excess fibre in diet (can cause diarrhoea, which stops oestrogen from being absorbed into gut)
- Deficiency of Vitamin A (needed for production of oestrogen)
- Antibiotics (stops absorption in gut)
- Over-exercising (affects tissues and circulation and can make you look older)
- Smoking (alters metabolism, which is why people who smoke tend to age quicker. Also linked to osteoporosis).

Falling oestrogen levels can cause symptoms such as

- Loss of temperature regulation (hot flushes)
- Memory deterioration
- Mood swings (including anger or inappropriate sex urges)
- Loss of muscle tone (e.g. causing prolapse of uterus or poor bladder control)
- Loss of vaginal tone
- Vaginal dryness
- Fatigue
- Ageing skin (crinkling around the mouth, sagging jaw lines)
- Weight gain (especially on hips and stomach)
- Loss of bone density
- Thinning hair
- Sleep disorders
- Bone disease such as osteoporosis.

A younger woman's understanding of the menopause

Meg, 42

I've recently come out the other side of a very difficult divorce, and I'm just beginning to feel youthful and joyous, so I don't really want to think about the menopause coming over the horizon. Anyway, my gynaecologist says my ovaries are full of eggs and I'm nowhere near menopausal.

I've never spoken to my mother about it. I know she had a hysterectomy, but she never talked about what happened to her as a consequence. Mind you, even my periods were shrouded in mystery. When I was sent to boarding school, she gave me a packet of pads and told me I would know what to do with them when the time came. I didn't have a clue what she was talking about.

What do I know about the menopause? Well, I kind of look at it as something I need to embrace at some point. I know there will be a change in hormones, and that women's minds become clearer – they start to think less emotionally, and more practically. I read that somewhere.

I'm also heartened to read about women continuing to have sex well into their seventies. I certainly won't like to think that my sex life is over. Sex is part of who you are as a woman. I've read about loss of libido in an agony column, but I take the view that there are loads of reasons why this could happen. Dreadful relationships don't do anything for your sex life for a start.

I have a couple of older friends who, because of their age, must have gone through it. They are stylish, elegant, lovely, vibrant women. I don't think about them as pre- or postmenopause, so that makes me think, don't be scared of it. I have no idea if they are taking anything though. I have never had that kind of conversation with them. In fact, I've never talked to friends of my own age about it either – I guess we are too busy bring up our families – or actually had a conversation with anyone about the way the body operates.

I think I'm good on acceptance. I know I'm going to grow older like everyone else, and one day pop my clogs. So, yes, I'm going to treat the menopause as an incident or event that will happen to my body at some point. I am expecting it to bring its own health issues and it will make me feel a bit older, but that's about it. I will carry on being the same person.

What would I like to see in this book? Clear, non-hysterical information, and the fact that the menopause is not the end of womanhood as I know it now. I would also like it to get rid of this notion that you cease to be sexually active, and attractive. That would be really good. In general, I would like to see the menopause being an accepted part of the female cycle. More everyday, and less of that Red Letter thing.

Mind you, since I don't know much about it, I might be talking nonsense. By the way, I've got a question for you. What *is* the difference between being fertile and coming to the end of childbearing years?

Introduction

Meg's question about coming to the end of childbearing years is a big one. Actually, it's about as big as it gets for women approaching the menopause. What happens to our body? What can we expect to feel when we say goodbye to our youth? How does our female identity change? What happens to our sexuality? How do we find a new sense of meaning and purpose? How *do* women today prepare for this life change?

It was quite a shock to realize that, although she's a generation younger than me, Meg is just as ignorant about the menopause as I was at her age. So, it set me thinking about what it has really been like for me, as a woman reaching the other side of such a huge transition (with the dust still settling), and how I might help Meg to understand what lies in store. What wise statement could I make to get the creative juices flowing?

And that's the nub of it. It's all about juices, or in my case, the lack of them.

Looking back, I now realize I must have been just about perimenopausal when I met the man who was to become my second husband. I was 48 at the time, he three years older. Like most newly met couples, we spent a lot of time tearing clothes off each other, thinking how wonderful it was to be this sexually active at our age.

Some time after we married, things began to change. I was around 52 by then, and I started to notice that my periods had become irregular. At the same time, I began to suffer from some pretty black headaches, but that was about it. I never experienced hot flushes. They were more like tepid glows. But in the sexual desire department there was most definitely a change, and this was affecting how I looked at life.

The first time I remember actively discouraging my husband's advances was on the Camino de Santiago pilgrim route across northern Spain. We don't choose beach holidays, so given that this happened in the middle of 12 days of hard cycling on our tandem, I put my lack of interest down to exhaustion and a sore bum.

When we returned home, I noticed that I still wasn't madly keen, but things seemed to settle down. Until, that is, I realized sex had became painful. For a while I pretended everything was okay. Finally, I had to confess that sex wasn't much fun any more. It wasn't an easy moment for either of us. 'This isn't what I signed up for,' said my husband, sitting in bed one Sunday morning, clutching a cup of tea and looking forlorn and cross. 'I'm not rejecting *you*,' I said hastily. 'It's just that my bits have gone on strike.' 'Humph,' he replied, throwing back the covers and stomping off to the bathroom.

I mentioned what I was going through to a couple of long-time friends. They looked horrified. 'What?! You don't want sex!?' said one. The other added helpfully, 'Well, you'd better watch out. There's plenty of younger women out there.' A conversation killer, and I was left feeling there was something wrong with me.

I began searching for information to make sense of what I was going through. On the psychology of the menopause, very little seemed to have moved on since 1991, when Germaine Greer wrote *The Change*, offering spirited advice on how to blow a raspberry at the ageing process, and how to accept that happiness is about inner serenity rather than outward appearance. It's still a great read and a fascinating historical look at attitudes of men and society towards the menopause. But it didn't resolve my curiosity to know how women of my own age were actually handling the real, lived experience of being menopausal.

Most of what else I found saw the menopause mainly as a medical problem in need of fixing, particularly the loss of libido and painful sex. There was little serious consideration of the enormous emotional and spiritual changes we women go through when our looks start to fade and our sense of meaning and purpose in life begins to shift.

So, I decided to talk to a female GP from the surgery. She looked so young I wanted to tuck her up in bed and tell her a bedtime story. I told her about sex being painful.

'Vaginal atrophy,' she said pityingly, her eyes firmly on the computer screen as she rattled out a prescription on her keyboard. Localized hormone replacement therapy cream (HRT) was what I needed, she said, to be inserted daily with a syringe. I was out of there in less than eight minutes.

I showed the tube to my husband, who, of course, was initially very pleased. I tried it for a couple of weeks, and we also tried to have sex again. But, I felt miserable about using it, so the tube ended up in the bin, and my husband resumed his former hangdog look. Having always used alternative medicine, I couldn't get my head round the idea of putting artificial hormones into my body, which, more than likely, were by-products of mares' urine collected from the poor things by a catheter. And, anyway, I was convinced that the cream was giving me the same kind of stomach cramps that sometimes used to happen just before my period. I admit this might have been psychosomatic, but it put me off completely.

My interest sparked off again when a friend suggested that natural progesterone cream made from wild yams might help. Following a hefty bill on my credit card, three months' supply arrived, and my husband's face lit up again. I faithfully applied it twice a day to various parts of my body. I felt good. In fact, I felt great. But it made not a jot of difference to my libido. I needn't describe my husband's face. I didn't bother to reorder.

This was around the time I was reading Elizabeth Gilbert's *Eat, Pray, Love*, an autobiographical account of a woman in her mid-30s in search of self-healing and romance. By the end of the book, Gilbert is spending a lot of time in enthusiastic sexual abandonment with her new lover. Her story may have inspired millions, but when I read that bit I thought cynically, 'When she's my age I bet she'll be wishing he'd get lost so she can enjoy a cup of tea in peace.'

This got me thinking. I seemed to be putting in a lot of time and effort into finding ways to have sex, not for my sake but for my husband's. *Was* I abnormal? No, I thought, there *must* be other women struggling with this as well. I began to drop the odd comment about menopause and sex into conversations with women who I thought might be open to talking about it.

Their response was amazing. Not only were they receptive, they seemed to be relieved that at last someone was mentioning the unmentionable. What encouraged me in particular was one woman who enthused, albeit in hushed tones, 'This is even more of a taboo than talking about dying.' That really struck a chord, because talking about dying is what my last book, *The D-Word*, was about. I realized the menopause is also a death, and that it creates the same intense feelings of denial, anger, guilt, confusion and eventual acceptance that happen during any painful bereavement. I knew I was onto something.

As my conversations with menopausal women continued, it was even more extraordinary to realize how many *men* wanted to talk about it. Crammed into a corner at a noisy Christmas party, one husband confessed to me that he had no idea how to broach the subject of sex with his wife now that she had gone through the menopause. He felt isolated from her, and was feeling tempted to look elsewhere. A shocking thought for him, having previously enjoyed a long and stable relationship.

It's no good being moralistic about this. It was how he felt. The sadness is that he didn't know who to turn to. Certainly, he had never spoken to another man about it. 'Would rather stick my head into a snake pit,' he muttered into his glass of wine.

So, I decided to grab the serpent by the tail and approach my fresh-faced 29-year-old male editor at Continuum Books.

'There's a guidebook that needs to be written for women and their partners explaining the emotional aspect of the menopause,' I told him, 'especially when it comes to sex, and finding meaning and purpose. You personally may not need the book now. But you will in the future. And so will your wife when you get one.' Much to my surprise, he asked for a proposal.

A few weeks later the proposal was ready for the all-important commissioning meeting. We spoke just before he went in, but he wasn't entirely convinced this would be up the street of his mostly male, 50-something bosses. 'That's okay,' I said. 'If they resist, ask them if they're still having enough sex. I bet they'll say no. So, tell them this book is as much for them as it is for their menopausal wives.'

I waited anxiously for his phone call, and was thrilled when it finally came. 'I couldn't quite find the courage to ask them if they were having enough sex,' my editor told me, 'but there was lots of droll comment and sniggering round the boardroom table. I cracked a few jokes, made a fool of myself, and amazingly, they went for it.'

What this book offers

I am an accredited psychotherapist, but I am not a doctor, menopause health professional or a sex therapist. So I am not setting myself up as an expert. This book is not an academic or medical study, and, although there are interviews with men and women from a range of socio-economic and cultural backgrounds, this isn't a multicultural examination of the menopause. Nor, indeed, is it a guide to getting your mojo back. It does not contain 'my personal fibroid stories', tell you what menopausal archetype you are, suggest you walk on hot coals as a purification ritual (although, come to think of it, that's quite an idea), or discuss ethical issues such as assisted conception for the older woman. These subjects are well catered for elsewhere. I'm not a radical feminist either, so this book is not about denouncing men or saying you should give up sex to save yourself from their predations.

So, what *is* the book about?

Above all, I want to challenge the notion that the menopause, the dreaded M-word, is a dysfunction in need of treatment. Menopause is a vastly more complex and rich transition than that. So this book goes into battle against how society regards the ageing process; tackles taboos about sex in later life; explores how meaning changes as we grow older; hears from men about what it's like to live with a menopausal woman; and confronts what I believe is often inadequate medical information about hormone replacement therapy (HRT).

This is guided by my own experience of being what I believe is a fairly typical just-short-of-60 woman, now morphing into a postmenopausal state, and undergoing all kinds of inward and outward changes that I could never have begun to imagine as a younger woman.

My journey has led me to meet and interview more than 70 women (straight and gay) about their attitudes to the menopause, the sexual changes they have experienced, how their relationships have been affected, the losses they have encountered, and the way they are making new meaning as older women living in an otherwise hyper-sexualized and youth-obsessed society.

I also interviewed nine remarkably generous and courageous men, married or partnered to menopausal women. Their frankness and openness touched me deeply. I hope their stories will not just help other couples understand the impact that the menopause can have on a marriage or partnership, but also provide a much broader perspective on what's involved when a woman reaches menopausal age.

Many of my interviewees had never spoken about the menopause before. Some had never even spoken about sex at all. Some felt relieved to give voice to the unmentionable; others found it uncomfortable, and, at times, painful. They all willingly agreed to talk, because they also wanted to challenge the taboos and assumptions that get in the way of most discussions that happen around sex, meaning and menopause. Given the sensitivity of these issues, the names of most of my interviewees have either been changed or left out.

I am aware that this book will probably pose more questions than it can answer, and how impossible it would be to cover every aspect of such a vast subject. I have therefore included, if you want to delve deeper, a list of recommended books and websites at the end.

I also know that in some ways this book speaks both to and about women (and men) who enjoy a relatively privileged lifestyle. Even in our Western societies, many older women are too concerned about daily survival, or caught up in family responsibilities, or financial pressures or physical or emotional illness and trauma to have the space or money to think more deeply about the menopause. My hope, though, is that this book goes some way towards honouring them too.

Structure

Sex, Meaning and the Menopause is divided into six chapters, dealing with different menopausal 'M-word' themes. Each of these can be read on its own, or in sequence as part of the whole book.

Chapter 1: Myth-Making sets out the messages that menopausal women receive in today's Western societies, and considers briefly how other cultures regard the menopause.

Chapter 2: Myth-Busting. Women talk about their *real* experience of the menopause, from the distress of fading beauty to finding a new sense of self.

Chapter 3: Menopausal Mechanics tackles taboos around sex, from the physiological and psychological changes that happen to how differently men and women experience this transition.

Chapter 4: Meaning explores the deeper spiritual and existential perspectives of menopause that can help women come to terms with their ageing process.

Chapter 5: Men and the Menopause! is a frank and moving collection of in-depth interviews with men married or partnered with menopausal women.

Chapter 6: Managing the Menopause gives what I hope is a different perspective on treatments for the menopause, such as HRT, as well as information on alternative approaches.

The book concludes with a suggested reading list and some useful websites.

Supported and encouraged by a lot of men, especially by my husband Mark (my very own M-word), I've aimed this book not just at women, but especially also at husbands and partners who are even less prepared than their wives and girlfriends, or indeed mothers and sisters, for the physical and existential changes that come with the menopause.

And while this is not an academic book, I hope the stories here will add a different, lived and *felt* dimension to research elsewhere that reduces the menopause to hard, dry facts about symptoms. For, as one interviewee commented, 'After starting your periods, this is *the* experience of a woman's life.'

A word about the male menopause

In Chapter 5, you will find several men referring to the male menopause. Before we go any further, let me clear up possible misunderstandings. Yes, men in their middle years and beyond do experience changes in their hormone levels. Some may not be able to maintain erections. Many go through an existential life crisis and wonder what life is all about. Others may become much more interested in younger women than they were. But a menopause in the literal, physical sense? No.

A recent research paper in the respected *New England Journal of Medicine* refers to the male menopause as 'late-onset hypogonadism', which basically means there's a lowering in testosterone levels in some men after midlife. But, the paper reminds us that men can't physically have a menopause. Quite simply, they do not possess a set of ovaries, and therefore do not experience the same almighty drop in hormone levels as we do.

'The fact is, guys,' wrote Pat Wingert and Barbara Kantrowitz (authors of *The Menopause Book*) in *Newsweek*,

[m]enopause is ours. We have earned it by enduring decades of menstrual periods, mood swings, and all the other inconveniences that come with being a woman. It wasn't always fun, but it was our life. For most women, menopause isn't just an end to all that; it's also a moment of psychological and emotional reckoning. When your periods stop, you know something has changed irrevocably in your body. You may exercise and watch your weight and use sunscreen every day to keep looking as young as possible. But inside, your body is

definitely aging. Women can't be in denial about that the way men can.

At the risk of sounding sexist, put that in your pipe and smoke it. Men as they approach midlife may end up chasing after women half their age, or roar about in red Ferraris. But for a woman, the menopause combined with the midlife crisis is a deeper and more complex transition. And that's what this book is about.

CHAPTER 1

Myth-making: menopause and society

Helmet haircut. Wobbling bat wings under upper arms. Thighs of lard. Clothes to terrify a landfill. Or, botoxed vamps who prey on innocent young men.

Both these stereotypes exist. But there are countless women in Western societies who, finding themselves like me somewhere between these two extremes, are desperately trying to maintain a psychological and spiritual balance as they go through the emotional, mental and physical upheaval of the menopause.

Today's menopausal women make up the tail end of the 1945–1955 generation of baby boomers born in the aftermath of the Second World War. When we were small, our mothers and grandmothers – like their own parents – toed the line, did their sexual duty and sold us a romantic dream. 'One day your prince will come, but in the meantime, don't even think about having sex before marriage.'

But of course most of us went on to do just that, while those of the older generation stood aside, shook their heads in disapproval, and watched us seemingly have it all: sexual liberation *and* emancipation. Financial stability *and* choice. Career *and* children.

The key word there is 'seemingly'. Yes, we've been through extraordinary social and cultural changes, but our hormones pay little attention to the shifting values of a celebrity-dominated culture obsessed with youth and beauty. Bang on time, as they have done the same way since we lived in caves, our bodies are responding to the natural order of things, and turning us into older women.

So, what is it *really* like to be menopausal in today's world?

I received wonderful support when I began to tell people about the idea for this book. Friends passed on the names of other friends willing to be interviewed, and I met more women through a number of workshops I ran as part of my research.

This is how Serena came into my life. She's an energetic, 53-year-old yoga teacher and networker *extraordinaire*. As soon as she heard what I was up to, she invited me to hold a workshop with a group of older women, all experienced therapists and alternative health practitioners. Most were in their mid to late 50s. Two were almost 70.

I started the day with a simple question, 'What does it feel like to be a menopausal woman in modern society?' This is some of what they came up with: Don't talk about it. It's not important/It doesn't happen. It's dangerous. It's ugly. I've lost the plot. I'm invisible. Non-status. Don't take part in big decisions any more. Loss of recognition. Change. Embarrassed to admit I don't want sex any more. Isolation. Shock. Uncertainty. Bewilderment. Does men-o-pause mean a pause from men?

If these intelligent women, specializing what's more in health and well-being, felt this negatively, how on earth does the woman in the street truly feel about herself, especially when it comes to learning to accept that life is never going to be the same once the menopause arrives?

Even so, as the day progressed and we really began to talk about what the menopause meant personally, it became clear that it was in fact anything but a purely negative experience. Some women said they also felt liberated, excited, much more creative and self-accepting. 'It's okay to be me,' said one. 'I like being selfish in a positive sense,' said another. A third said she was enjoying moving out of the role of mother, and becoming more of a mentor. 'I like spending more time out in the world as who *I* am, rather who I am expected to be.' Others saw it as a chance to revisit hopes and dreams, and to reassess what mattered to them. One participant said she now understood how she had, as it were, made the bed in which she now had to lie.

> At the same time, I'm aware I still need to change the sheets on a regular basis. There's no point hankering after a past that never happened. I sometimes mourn for the years that I never lived – my early life was more like survival – and I know I have aches and pains to look forward to. But I am learning to see that any future choices I make will be from a place of wisdom that has been hard won.

I really resonated with what this participant said about turning life experiences into wisdom. It made me even more aware of the menopause as *the* psychological watershed of a woman's life. However, most information currently out there seems to focus on physical symptoms, especially when it comes to the loss of libido. And I'm fed up with it. So, thankfully, is Ray Moynihan, Australian health journalist and author of *Sex, Lies and Pharmaceuticals*. He says that female 'sexual dysfunction' has been invented by the pharmaceutical industry to generate global drug markets to treat it.

As we will discover from interviewees throughout this book, women's relationship with sex, particularly as they reach the menopause, is far more complicated than being reduced to a disorder for the financial benefits of drug companies.

The focus on sex

When it comes to the menopause, we are bombarded by messages from society saying all that matters is sex. While I appreciate that many menopausal women are very keen to continue to have sex – and they have every right to do so – I'm left with the message that if I don't, there's something wrong with me. This makes me furious. As I see it, my oestrogen levels have fallen, just as they're meant to, and my body is naturally responding to the end of my life as a fertile woman. Granted this isn't much fun for my husband, but it's not something I want to have 'fixed'. I would like to move into the next stage of my life as an older woman, hopefully putting the wisdom of a hard-lived life to good use, both at home and at work. As I see it, this has nothing to do with whether I want sex or not.

Then again, there is doubt. *Is* there something wrong with me? Am I less of a person and a woman because my libido has taken a dive? Would my spiritual development suffer if I gave in and had HRT. As I write this, I can feel my soul screaming, Yes! It *would* indeed be a spiritual sacrifice. But the question that causes me most distress is: Am I being selfish? I may not be that interested in sex any more, but I am married and this means I am denying another human being his sexuality as well.

When it also involves the welfare of someone else, especially when you love them very much, remaining true to the call of one's soul can be difficult. This conflict has made me ask why our modern culture ignores these deeper, challenging issues.

Menopause: a medical diagnosis

To understand, we need to look at how we learn about the menopause. Most of what women today have read about this transition sits firmly within a Western scientific and medical tradition. This might be termed as a masculine, logical approach which, it seems to me, has all but banished the softer, more nebulous feminine qualities of sensitivity, intuition and creativity. We're given the facts about physiological changes in a woman's body, but seldom any recognition of the deep, inward transformation she often goes through at the same time. Therefore, rather than the menopause being seen as a holistic experience, and a woman's natural transition, worthy of respect, out of one life stage into another, Western science has come to view our bodies as fundamentally a piece of equipment, with 'symptoms' to be treated or corrected. True, that's allowed doctors to deduce and diagnose physical disease and dysfunction. But it's not an approach that recognizes or trusts the deeper spiritual or existential essence of human nature.

Hot flushes and declining libido are certainly physical indicators that hormone levels are falling. But as Marilyn Glenville points out in her book *Natural Alternatives to HRT*, some 'menopausal' symptoms such as joint pain, lack of energy and ageing skin affect men of the same age just as much. In addition, symptoms such as anxiety or loss of self-esteem can also relate to significant life events that have nothing to do with falling hormone levels. Glenville goes on,

> The classic example of this is the 'empty nest syndrome' which many women have to face up to in their late 40s or early 50s when children leave home. This can be quite a crisis. To try to explain away these powerful and legitimate feelings in terms of falling hormone levels is to dismiss many women's important experiences of motherhood.

Drugs for sex

So it's time to climb onto my soapbox.

Not only does science fall short in the way it portrays different types of 'menopausal' symptoms, it also places considerable emphasis on negative sexual changes, such as vaginal dryness, loss of libido and a decrease in the ability to orgasm. Remarkably little research considers how these sexual changes can also be positive for many women, as we will hear in Chapter 3.

In fact, Professor Julie Winterich, an American feminist sociologist, told me that Western attitudes towards the menopause are fuelled by research that focuses on *whether* women experience sexual changes rather than *how* women view changes in their sex lives.

Winterich discovered through her own research into sex and the menopause that when women were invited to talk about their personal experiences of the sexual changes they were going through, they provided a much broader range of positive responses. 'Many women,' she told me, 'said they had never spoken about it with anyone before. Some found it uncomfortable, but also said how good it felt to talk about it.'

Negative messages about sexual dysfunction are alarming on two counts. First, they work against a woman adjusting to a different state of being as an older person, whether she remains sexual or not. Second, – as already noted – they feed into a massive moneymaking machine for the pharmaceutical industry.

An example is Viagra. Introduced in 1998 for the treatment of male erectile problems, Viagra has become the best-selling prescription drug of all time. However, Meika Loe, Assistant Professor of Sociology and Women's Studies at Colgate University, and author of *The Rise of Viagra*, points out that Viagra is being marketed to ageing men whose wives and partners are also going through sexual changes – sometimes crisis – brought about by the menopause.

These women want less sex but their partners now want more. Isn't this counter-intuitive? Doesn't this turn the bedroom into a battlefield at a time when women are already vulnerable (e.g. empty nest syndrome, feeling less attractive as we age, physical changes due to menopause including hair loss and weight gain, etc.)

Others worry about the social implications of these drugs. The Viagra myth, says Dr Abraham Morgentaler, author of a book of the same name, has less to do with the effectiveness of the medication than with our cultural desire to look for an easy fix.

Many of my male patients, together with many of their partners, came to realize that finally achieving a great erection did not solve their relationship problems. In fact, it frequently made them worse. Sometimes when the erection issue is solved, couples are forced to deal with more profound troubles in the relationship.

For many menopausal women, the traditional 'easy fix' for the menopause is HRT. Various forms of hormone replacement therapy have been used since the 1950s to prevent menopausal symptoms and to boost the sex lives of older women. HRT is often sensitively recommended for women in their 30s and 40s who have had a hysterectomy or are taking anti-cancer medication. But many women have used HRT as a lifestyle choice to avoid the ageing process. Nonetheless, these hormonal treatments only delay the menopause, and there are health risks associated with using it long-term. (I will be going into women's experiences of HRT in Chapter 6.)

There is also a growing wave of publications such as *The Hormone of Desire: The Truth about Sexuality, Menopause and Testosterone* by psychiatrist Dr Susan Rako, where testosterone therapy is promoted as a major breakthrough for women reaching midlife. Rako maintains that testosterone, taken in small doses, can be highly effective in restoring general well-being, sexual libido and a return to a 'normal' life. She believes that as life expectancy has increased so dramatically no woman reaching the menopause should suffer the loss of sexual desire.

To deliver this testosterone fix, new treatments are constantly coming onto the market, for example, a controversial patch by the name of *Intrinsa*. At the time of writing, this has been approved for use in Europe but not in the US. There is also *Flibanserin*, which apparently lifts inhibitions as well as being a mood enhancer. Originally this drug was developed to alleviate depression.

All this sounds good, but there's a dark side. Side effects of testosterone can include hair loss, breast pain, weight gain, insomnia, changes to voice, and migraines. And, goodness knows what these 'curatives' do to our spirit.

There's another matter of concern. Arlene Weintraub, science and technology writer for *Business Week* who spent four years researching the anti–ageing industry for her book, *Selling the Fountain of Youth*, says that people are using such large amounts of these anti-ageing hormones, often as prescribed as skin creams, that their partners are absorbing it just by lying next to them at night.

Sure, hormone treatments can artificially stimulate our libido, but they *cannot* return us to the 'normal' life of the fertile woman we once were. Those days are gone. One woman I interviewed was particularly infuriated by these messages:

Evolution naturally takes away our fertility at the menopause.
That's why women's libido falls. It's meant to. This isn't recognized.
Instead science sees it as a failure, which needs to be fixed. I find this
unacceptable.

So do I.

To me, it seems that science and the media are conspiring to redefine what life is. Their message yells, 'You can't be regarded as youthful – or even fully alive – if you're not sexual.' I see this as a fundamental abuse of what it means to be human and grow old. It leaves me feeling frustrated, invisible and unheard, as well as outraged by how drug companies are taking advantage of women at this enormously sensitive time in our lives.

Fortunately, others are also calling for change. When American film producer Liz Crammer began to make erotic videos for a drug company which was developing an 'orgasm cream' to boost women's sex lives, she realized just how much women were being exploited. She says in an interview with *The Mail Online*, 'The whole idea of these drugs is twisted. It's not about sexual empowerment for women; it's about exploiting women and making billions in profits for drug companies.' Crammer's resulting film, *Orgasm Inc.*, exposes how drug companies and doctors are locked in a race to produce a 'female Viagra', that promises women a super-charged sex life in pill form.

I realize this may be slightly deviating from the point, but I did laugh when I found that we now even have a National Orgasm Day. Orgasm Day was launched in 2008 by SPM Ltd, a small company that manufactured the Pelvic Toner, a medical device to reduce stress incontinence. Following the suggestion by Professor Emmanuelle Jannini, an endocrinologist from the University of L'Aquila, Italy, that, no matter what age, most women cannot achieve a vaginal orgasm because they lack a G-spot, the company realized that orgasm was far sexier than incontinence. So it counterattacked by saying, of course women, young and old, have G-spots. They just needed to invest in the Pelvic Toner to make themselves more sensitive to stimulation. So, welcome to Orgasm Day, a momentous annual event which, let's face it, is a lot more to do with flogging sex aids that it is about providing intelligent sex education, or indeed, relevant information to older women.

The anti-ageing lobby

Staying on my soapbox, I despair equally at the way we are assailed with messages from the cosmetics industry. Professor Julie Winterich, who we met earlier, conducted a study in 2007 into what appearance changes mean to gay and heterosexual American women going through the menopause. She agrees that women are bombarded with advertising that tells them to 'fight the ageing process'.

In 2007, anti-ageing products and services, including weight-loss programmes, were estimated to gross 56 billion dollars in the US alone. Some estimated this figure would rise to 88 billion dollars by 2010. Winterich told me, 'The images produced by the cosmetics industry normalize cultural ideas about attractiveness based on young, white, thin, heterosexual, middle-class people, even though the US population is aging, and is diverse by race, ethnicity and class.'

Some female celebrities are turning to very dubious practices in their desperation to retain their youth. Recently, 47-year-old Australian supermodel Elle Macpherson admitted to using the horn of endangered rhinoceroses to maintain a smooth skin. I believe she takes it in powder form.

Fifty-seven-year-old Sharon Osborne, co-host of *America's Got Talent*, confessed on a British television programme to spending a hefty £120,000 on her face and body over the years. She maintains that most female celebrities over the age of 30 have started to use cosmetic surgery to preserve their looks and figure. However – and hurrah for them – there are older celebrities and actresses who are making a stand against the practice, such as British actress Jacqueline Bisset, now in her 60s. Bisset says she thinks 'women who had plastic surgery looked like freaks'.

Channel 4's 2010 series *The Ugly Face of Beauty* was a reminder how the search for physical beauty can end up as a horror story. The programme graphically illustrated what can go wrong when, for example, a woman of 40 believes surgical implants will return her breasts to the shape of a 20-year-old's. This is simply impossible, not to mention the risk of scarring or the need for further corrective surgery when operations haven't gone to plan.

And now you can buy face-fillers such as Botox at the dentist. But what woman in her right mind would want to be injected with deadly botulinum toxins (or rat poison) when it's too early to know about long-term effects? Too many, it would seem.

Amy, a 50-year-old psychotherapist, summed up for me how

in her eyes, Western culture's focus on external beauty stops older women from becoming wise members of the community.

> When a woman reaches the menopause, she stops giving off those pheromones, and, sure, men aren't so interested any more. But we have other roles to step into as mature women. I think we *should* become the protectors and guardians of younger people's lives. Instead we are ignored.
>
> Western attitudes mean that we have little opportunity to pass on our knowledge – it's all about youth culture and making money. But when you look around and hear what's going on, you discover how lost most people are, especially younger women. They haven't got a clue about themselves, or how to use their femininity other than sexually.

Cultural differences

This constant pressure to stay looking and acting young prompted me to find out how representative British women's experiences are of the menopause. I was astounded to learn in an international study published in *Climateric*, the Journal of the International Menopause Society, that women in the UK probably have the world's worst menopause. The study also recognized that this finding could say as much about the quality of life of older women in the UK as it does about clinical signs of the menopause. Quality of life in the study refers to recognition and respect.

I asked Professor Lorraine Dennerstein from Melbourne University, Australia, about her research into cultural attitudes towards the menopause. She agreed that societies responded differently, especially when it comes to attitudes towards sex.

> Our research shows those women who live in Northern European countries, like Germany and the UK, and who come from cultures that don't value sex particularly highly, are less bothered about declining sexual function. However, when you talk to French or Spanish women who come from cultures that value sex, they are much more likely to be distressed.

All the women I interviewed for this book were either British-born or have lived in the UK most of their lives, so I can't compare the state of their libidos with those from hotter European countries. However, I spoke to my Danish friend, Karin, who thought the general British attitude towards the menopause was negative and restrictive. In her culture, it's accepted for grandmothers, mothers and daughters to spend time together, and to go to saunas as a regular family outing. 'It's no big deal. We see each other's naked bodies and think nothing of it,' she told me. 'The menopause is generally regarded as just another progression in a woman's life. Mind you, Scandinavians generally are much more open about sex and ageing anyway.'

I also spoke to Setsu, a very beautiful 60-year-old Japanese woman, married to her English husband for over 30 years, about the way she experiences English and Japanese attitudes towards the menopause.

She told me that the Japanese don't have a specific word for menopause. Rather, they refer to the phase of a woman's life between the ages of 40 and 60 as *konenki*. The word loosely means renewal and regeneration, with the end of menstruation being part of a natural transition. Therefore, *konenki* is regarded as a time when a woman over 40 tends to lose balance both biologically and culturally. However, as she passes through to the other side of *konenki* she begins to establish a new sense of herself. This different psychological approach may be why Japanese women appear to experience far fewer menopausal symptoms than Western women, and why many are not bothered by the menopause at all. Setu told me,

> We recognize *konenki* as an important time in a woman's life, especially these days. Traditionally Japan has had a terrible attitude towards older women. In my mother's generation, by the time she was forty she was considered old. This is changing with the baby boomers like myself. We are much more powerful, and take far more care of ourselves. We also talk to each other, so we are prepared for what's coming.

I asked Setu how she viewed British women's experience of the menopause.

> Here in the UK I don't think women look after themselves at all. They often leave it too late. For example, you can't expect everything to be alright just because you've suddenly started eating soya. Your body isn't accustomed to it.
>
> One of the reasons why Japanese women aren't bothered so much by symptoms is because of eating such a healthy diet from the time we are born, and we know that this helps us to prepare for *konenki*.

I love the concept of *konenki* as a culturally determined time frame in which a woman approaching menopause learns to accept what's happening to her, and has the opportunity – and understanding – that this is a time of renewal and regeneration. It's much softer and more allowing than how we interpret menopause in the West.

Other Asian societies also have a different psychological approach to the menopause. For example, in India, a Hindu woman who has a period cannot take part in religious ceremonies for the first four days of her cycle, nor is she allowed to cook. When she reaches the menopause, she is released from these taboos, and is treated with more respect (providing her husband stays alive) within the wider community. This means Hindu women tend to have a more positive attitude towards their ageing process, and, I understand, can even look forward to it.

Returning to Western society, a 1999 US study carried out on women's different cultural and racial attitudes towards the menopause and ageing suggested that ethnic groups such as Asians and Hispanics in America are more negative towards the menopause. The study argues that this directly contradicts the traditionally positive experiences of elder women within these communities. As with so much else, this seems to confirm how the focus on what you look like rather than who you are damages our inbuilt and evolutionary spiritual perceptions of life.

African Americans, according to the same study, were the most positive about the menopause. Black women were brought up to be strong and accepting of the ageing process, and in the context of other emotional, practical and cultural difficulties they faced, they tended to treat the menopause as just another part of life. However, the study does acknowledge that factors other than cultural context, such as personal background, medical history or coping mechanisms affect the way a woman individually experiences her menopause.

Professor Adele Green, an epidemiologist at the Queensland Institute of Medical Research in Brisbane, Australia, and at Manchester University, agrees.

It's important to remember that we are shaped by the family we are born into, our neighbourhood, our society, culture and traditions. Menstruation history also needs to be taken into account. For example, if a woman has suffered from premenstrual tension, she's more likely to have a difficult menopause.

Another factor is assessing how each individual woman may be affected by the thought of ending her reproductive years. How she's coping with the knowledge she isn't ovulating any more, what this means to her, and how she manages the understanding that she is no longer young.

All these issues will have an impact on a woman's attitude towards her sexuality and the way she experiences the menopause.

A Second Menopause? God forbid!

Menopause is enough of a challenge when it arrives during mid-life, but I was perturbed to read a report about experiments on female mice, which means we could experience a second one in our 80s. Dr Noriko Kagawa, assistant director of the Kato Ladies Clinic in Tokyo, has been transplanting ovarian tissue into older female mice to extend their life expectancy by more than 40 per cent. Dr Kagawa noted that the effects of the transplant wore off slowly, and the mice experienced a normal second menopause before they died. She does, however, think that human bodies will indeed finally wear out around 120 years old, whatever is done to them.

Having gone through the menopause, I am at a loss to know why I would want to go through it again just for the sake of adding a few more years to the end of my life. As far as I am concerned, the whole point of the menopause is to enable me to face my ageing process and to help me become more accepting of my mortality. No matter what I do to extend my life, as Dr Kagawa admits, the fact that I am going to die *is* inescapable.

Apart from feeling very sorry for the mice, it also makes me wonder about the quality of life we would endure after our second menopause, and to question what purpose and meaning we could contribute to society after a certain point. Not to mention the global problem of rapidly rising population numbers, the resulting destruction of our environment, and who is going to pay for us to dribble on into extreme old age in our bath chairs just because science says we can and should.

This chapter has looked at how science and medicine as well as Western myths about the menopause have little time, compassion, or respect for this being such a significant transition in a woman's life. In the next chapter, we're going to bust open these myths to hear women talking about what it's really like to go through it.

CHAPTER 2

Myth-busting: real, lived experiences

The first myth I want to confront is that of the menopause as a medical condition that's over and done with once your periods have stopped for 12 months. That's the same as saying you're suddenly a mature, sensible adult just because you've turned 18.

The second myth ripe for demolition is the idea that our 50s are the new 30s. This is *not* true. When a woman reaches her 50s, she enters a time of immense physical and psychological change. As Lesley Kenton writes in *Passage to Power*, it's a transition from young woman to older woman that can last up to ten years. And, of course, while there are a lot of common experiences that women share, each of us deals with the menopause in a completely different way. I've said it before, and let me say it again: the menopause is much more than a simply defined collection of medical symptoms.

Clinically, I became postmenopausal at the age of 54. Compared to some, I didn't have many physical problems, apart the loss of my libido (the next chapter looks at the mechanics of sexual change in much greater detail), but I certainly wasn't prepared for the grieving process I entered into, or how long it would take to come to some kind of acceptance that I was no longer a young woman. Some days I would look at my reflection in the mirror and feel utterly inconsolable, terrified to know I couldn't control what was happening to my face and body. At other times, I felt a much deeper shift going on, as if I was being pulled forward into a different way of relating to world, where I didn't yet know the rules.

The nearest experience I can compare it to was the strange feeling I had straight after my father died, my mother having died several years before. For weeks after his death, I had the sensation of being, whether I wanted to or not, energetically hauled up the generational ladder, to take my place as a matriarch.

I realized only recently that I had at last finally accepted that I was an older woman. It was at a friend's fiftieth birthday party where I was one of the oldest of some 20 female guests. Most were just approaching 50, or perhaps a year or so younger. Looking around the table, I guessed most of them were still menstruating. Their hair was glossy and thick, their skin still smooth, their bodies still shaped by soft feminine curves. I'm not saying I regarded myself as any less of a woman, but I realized I truly had stepped onto another level – the postmenopausal level. I felt suddenly both wistful and wise.

Sitting with these perimenopausal women also made me question how different it might have been if someone had warned me that the menopause was about much more than just the end of my periods, and that I was going to spend most of my 50s negotiating my way through such an emotional minefield.

Several women I interviewed for this book wondered whether it's really possibly to prepare oneself properly. Ruth, who took part in one of my Sex, Meaning and Menopause workshops, said that, looking back, she would have appreciated being told she was entering a time of complex change, rather than being given, as she put it, just the lists of symptoms that most books and websites provide. 'But the problem is,' she added, 'you don't start to think about the menopause until you have it.' How true. Rather like childbirth or divorce, you can have an intellectual idea of what might happen, but the actual experience will always be different, deeper and more personal.

So, for the rest of this chapter, we hear from women about those very personal experiences of their 50s, and the changes the menopause has brought. Some talk of the pain of losing their looks, while others mourn in particular the end of their fertility. Some talk of the challenge of caring for elderly parents, or of children leaving home, and one describes the struggle of being the menopausal mother of a child under ten, the result of a first and entirely unplanned pregnancy at the age of 48. Others talk of the loneliness of living by themselves, and some, as they approach retirement, of the change of working identity.

We'll begin with 55-year-old Christine, who had been aware of the menopause since her early 40s. She told me she'd also read a good deal about it, but the reality turned out to be very different.

It started when I was caring for a young woman of 40 who had leukaemia. Even though I knew her death was inevitable, when she died I was overwhelmed with a sense of loss and grief.

I realized it wasn't just about her, because suddenly I recognized that huge changes were coming towards me as well. It's as if her death stripped away any denial in me. My children had just left home, and my husband, who was also my business partner and 20 years older than me, was about to retire. This meant closing down the company. It threw me into turmoil. Who was I without all these familiar things around me?

Vivian was also completely unprepared for how she would feel after her children left home. She described it as 'living in a vacuum'.

I don't have grandchildren, so there's nothing to fill the child gap. Not that I particularly want it to. I thought about getting a dog, and then realized I didn't want the responsibility.

My life isn't empty. I have my partner, but this isn't about him, it's about me. I have been used to filling my life, running a home, bringing up children, having the business, and now I have a lot of time on my hands.

But I don't feel driven any more, and I find it difficult to access energy to create new things like I used to. It's a weird place to be, because part of me wants the space and quiet, while another part of me thinks, 'You're going to end up a lazy fat old woman.'

Christine compared her overall readiness for the menopause to that of bringing home her first baby from hospital.

I can remember looking at the baby and thinking, 'Help! What on earth do I do now?' You know what's coming when you're pregnant, but at the same time you haven't got a clue, because you've never had a baby before. It's the same with the menopause. I knew about it, but I had no idea what it entailed. It's been a complete shock.

Verity, in her 50s, also felt the same sense of chaos, and was struggling with her self-image.

I'm sure everything I have experienced until now has contributed hugely to who I am, but my menopause seems to be such a time of chaos and inner turmoil that I can't see where I am heading at the moment. Luckily I am wise enough to know this too will pass.

I'm not the kind of person, either, who goes on crash diets or works out at the gym for hours on end to try and carve away that extra flesh. I hate the extra weight I've put on. I'm a dancer, and I've always been proud of my figure, and the way I've been so flexible. Now I can't get up from the floor without pushing down with my hands. I've also had to completely change the colours and styles of my clothes, and I've also had to start colouring my hair regularly. I can't bear to go grey yet. I'm just not ready for that, or getting used to this new image of myself as an older woman.

I just want to add that I *have* chosen to go grey haired. This, by the way, was against the advice of the hairdresser I was going to at the time I made the decision. He was appalled at the thought. But, as I totted up the amount of money and time I have spent dying my hair since I was 40, I realized I didn't want to do it any more. I wanted to accept all the implications of growing older, including what was happening to my appearance. Looking at women of my own age, I am certainly in the minority, and I've received a mixed reaction. Some people can't understand why I'm happy to be grey. Others, including my husband, are very complimentary.

Fading beauty

For many women I interviewed, one of the most shocking changes (to me as well) is realizing that you've become all but invisible to most men.

Fellini's 1963 whimsical Oscar-winning film, 8½, harshly dramatizes the systemic shift from golden beauty to older woman. Guido, the middle-aged hero of the piece, fantasises about visiting his own harem and ends up whipping upstairs a woman approaching 60 to join all the other women who had gone beyond beauty and sexual prowess.

'I still deserve to be loved at 60,' wails the woman.

'You know the rules,' chorus the younger women as they continue to attend to Guido, knowing that one day this too will be their fate.

It's a powerful metaphor for what happens in many parts of the world. For example, in some Muslim cultures, younger wives are brought in as the first wife ages. And yet, in our own culture I can only imagine the outrage and pain I would feel if my husband brought home wife number two, or three for that matter. But, returning to Fellini's film, I did find a message of hope. Although the older women may have been hidden away, they were spoken of with warmth and respect by those still in the harem. The younger women knew that these benign characters were waiting for them, open-armed, with compassion and love. Therefore, as the banished woman stumbles up the stairs to be received by a kindly female attendant, rather than despair I felt a sense of relief for her. Older women make wonderfully prudent, humorous companions for each other.

A woman can only find real beauty once she has ceased the struggle to *be* beautiful, says Germaine Greer in *The Change*. 'She can at last transcend the body that was what other people principally valued for her, and be set free both from their expectations and her own capitulation of them.'

I agree with Greer. But first we have to face the pain and despair of being 'whipped upstairs'. Personally, I can't remember a particular moment when it happened, but one day, I realized I had quite simply lost the ability to 'pull'. It was devastating. I've just about got used to it now, but 53-year-old Lizzie was still devastated when we spoke.

> I always enjoyed going to clubs, although I haven't been for quite a while. But I went out with a friend the other night, and it was horrible to realize something had gone. That was very obvious when a man tapped me on the shoulder. I turned round, but he said 'sorry' and walked away.
>
> From the back I obviously looked far younger than I did in the front. It threw me into a downward spiral. I like being a woman. I love my sexuality and the intricacies of being female. But who am I when my looks are gone?

Melissa is also in her early 50s. She too has had to face the fact that men aren't attracted to her as they used to be.

> These days I look at myself as someone whose leaves are falling, and spring isn't coming again. I have to acknowledge that talking to men has become like having a polite conversation. There's no edge to it. I used to be very good at flirting. It was how I got my kicks. The loss is dreadful.

Fifty-seven-year-old Dana was a little further down the road of acceptance.

> When you know you've caught a man's attention, it gives you the most incredible buzz that goes beyond sex. It talks directly to the part

of your brain that goes, 'Woo-hey! I'm queen bee.' It's crushing when
it stops.

    Now I'm menopausal I realize everything's about oestrogen. When
that goes, it's the end of being a sexually alluring woman. I think
that's why so many women find this change so difficult. It's knowing
deep down that we're no longer of biological use.

Jennifer, a 56-year-old restaurateur, was very philosophical when she
told me how she had learnt to hold onto what's left.

I know I can't change it, and I have no control over it. Yes,
underneath, I hate losing control over my body. But I'm learning to
accept this unenviable process with as much grace as I can. I used to
dress very provocatively. I still have my moments, but I do try not to
look like mutton dressed up as lamb, and to stop myself behaving
like an idiot.

Anita, in her late 50s, also told me how painful it was to say goodbye
to physical youth. She was particularly sensitive to the way older
women were portrayed in the media.

A lot of older actresses are exposed in the media, and I don't think
that's right or fair. Nor is the controversy over sacking older female
television presenters. None of us – male or female – will escape the
ageing process. But it's very difficult for a woman to turn it into a
positive when the media can be so cruel.

Anita, herself, had come to the point where she found her own ageing process funny rather than hurtful.

I can be treated as if I'm invisible, but these days it only amuses me.
One of my daughters sent me a wonderful card about it. It was an
image of an ageing woman walking through customs with a cannabis
plant on her head, and none of the male customs officers were
taking a blind bit of notice. It made me laugh a lot.

Sixty-year-old Billie had also come to terms with her new status.

There is a completely different set of rules when you're a
menopausal woman. For a start, you've no longer got the cards
in your hand which enabled you to relate sexually. So it's about

finding other tactics instead, such as personality, or whatever. Trouble is, you have to realize you're on borrowed time. As soon as a younger woman appears, men will be round her like flies. There's no point getting upset about it, it's just male evolutionary programming.

The other day I had this very experience with the evolutionary perspective of the male at a work-related lunch. I was sitting next to a charming man in his early 50s. We were having a thoroughly pleasant conversation about his job, when the chair next to a very attractive younger woman became vacant on another table. He politely drew the conversation to a close, and was gone in a flash. Fortunately, I am now at the stage where I can smile when these things happen. But I was equally aware that, in the old days, it would have been me to whom he would have been paying court.

Fifty-six-year-old Mary took a very pragmatic view of what's happened to her.

> I certainly wouldn't describe myself as someone's who's lost it. It's up to you to make the best of what's going on.
>
> Yes, I've looked in the mirror and seen the changes. But these don't happen overnight. It's a gradual process. Some of us might be clinging on to youth through plastic surgery and hormone replacement therapy. But at some point, you *do* stop turning heads. It happens to us all.
>
> This doesn't mean that people have to ignore you. It's up to you to keep being noticed in a different way. That could be through your work, or perhaps becoming a wise person within your family situation. The menopause is a time to reassess things, and do them differently.

We've heard about fading beauty, but as some women pointed out, becoming a wise person within the family unit is not necessarily the easiest thing to do when teenagers are knocking about – particularly when it comes to daughters.

Mothers and daughters

I have two sons, so I don't know what it's like to go through the menopause with an adolescent daughter in the house. From one interviewee, I gathered that this can be quite an experience. 'A menopausal woman living with a pubescent daughter,' she said, through clenched teeth, 'is nothing less than the work of the devil.'

Other mothers seemed to have had a more peaceful time with their daughters. One told me how much she was enjoying 'passing on the mantle of womanhood'. Another was very proud of the way she and her daughter were coming out of a difficult time and beginning thoroughly to enjoy each other's company.

However, several women spoke to me about the complexity of confronting their ageing process at the same time their daughters were often turning into beautiful young women. One postmenopausal woman said it was like living with a mirror that she could never escape. Sheila, whose daughter is 17, found it equally uncomfortable.

> I have a beautiful daughter. That's becoming increasingly obvious when we are out together. It used to be me who got the whistles, and now it's her. It throws you into a massive learning curve. I know I am older and it pisses me off that I haven't got the maturity to deal with it properly – or better than I do anyway.
>
> No-one tells us what it will feel like when we reach this time of our lives. It's a very serious stage in the role of woman and mother. I want my legacy to be of benefit to my daughter so she can feel whole and safe. I didn't as a child. My mother was very abusive to me, so I want to do it differently with my daughter.

Janet has experienced similar feelings as her 15-year-old daughter matures.

> There are certain situations that are forcing me to face the fact that I am not a young woman any more. It's a feeling of redundancy. My son has left home, and my daughter is becoming a woman. She's up and coming, and I'm decreasing. That's very painful for me.

Some find it a relief

For some interviewees, the transition from sexual diva into someone who is almost invisible to men was a relief. In fact, to me it seemed that they gave a completely new meaning to the phrase 'sexual liberation'.

Anne-Marie is a 53-year-old alternative health practitioner.

In my teens I was the classic long-blond-haired attractive teenage. I received overwhelming attention from men, and I used to get into dreadful trouble being a flirt. Actually, I was incapable of having a friendship with a man without sleeping with him. It always ended in explosive arguments and upsets.

Rather than feeling sad about losing that edge, I feel relief. I still regard myself as an attractive, vibrant person, but I don't have to worry about whether a man finds me attractive any more. It also means I can have really good intimate relationships with men which aren't sexual. I can't *tell* you what a release that is.

Sixty-year-old Sally agrees. As a young woman she was constantly harassed by men.

I couldn't walk down a street, or look at a view, or read a plaque on a wall without some wretched man popping up from somewhere. I remember someone wolf-whistled at me when I was eight months pregnant with the twins. When I turned round he was so mortified he covered his face with his hands!

Of course it's all very flattering and validating, and yes, you do miss it at first. But there are other things that are more important, like being a good role model for my daughters, and enjoying the work I do mentoring young people. Many of them have problems with their own mothers, so I can step in as 'good mother' until they work out how to have a better relationships at home. So, yes, for me these days, it's about becoming that wise woman.

Easier transition for some

Others said they weren't bothered by losing their looks at all. Sixty-one-year-old Liz, happily married for over 30 years, accepted she had never attracted that much male attention, and believed the transition into being an older woman had been easier for her because of it.

I've never been beautiful, and the room certainly never stopped when I walked into it. So nothing has changed for me.

I saw it happen to other women often enough – and, of course, I would have liked it to have happened to me. But you can't make it happen. You have to get used to knowing that you will never be able to trade on being stunning. I used my brain instead and had a successful career as a solicitor. But I imagine it must be very hard on women who have been used to attracting that amount of attention, and then it goes.

Diana also knew she would never be able to trade on her looks as a young woman. She is now in her early 60s, has been married twice (once divorced and once widowed) and has been with her present partner for five years.

> I never had a beautiful face, and I never will have. I knew that very early on. I had long hair, big hands and feet, a lousy complexion and a deep voice. I liked it when I became a mother because I finally felt I wore a label which said, 'This is a woman.'
>
> But I don't think it's got that much to do with external looks anyway. My second husband, who sadly died, thought I was the most beautiful thing that ever walked, which meant I felt wonderful when I was married to him. My present partner says the same, so I feel as attractive now as I've ever done. It's all about personality for me. The most important thing is that people like me, and I'm nice to them. Mind you, I've always looked after my body by exercising and eating well. I believe that makes you sparkle. I also make sure my shoulders are back and I look people in the eye – much more important than having your eyebrows plucked.

End of fertility

Fading beauty is unquestionably a very big issue for women, but many interviewees I spoke to were also deeply affected by their menstruation cycle coming to an end.

Fifty-two-year-old Brigitte is the mother of two adult children. She's been divorced for several years and recently met a new partner. She pretends that she still has periods. 'I don't want to own the fact I'm not a whole woman any more,' she said, 'and I certainly don't want him to think so either.'

> I know I have no control over what's happening to my body, but when my periods stopped I had this huge loss, of not feeling truly connected to myself any more. The tragedy is that I never realized what I had until it went. And, whatever miracle medicines are available, there's no potion or pill or quick fix for this. What happens inside you is irretrievable and irreplaceable.

Four years on, Jane, whose periods stopped when she was 48, is still finding it difficult to come to terms with what has happened to her body.

> I found it so upsetting that I turned it into a positive experience by saying I was free from having to take birth control any more. But underneath I know I am raging and grieving. I am grieving for the loss of power I had as a young woman. It's as if something inside me has died. I hate that.

Belinda, in her mid-50s, is heartbroken to know she will never have any more children.

> There is a grieving process that flickers in and out of my life. I look at a baby and know I can't have another one. You never know when it's going to be too late to have that choice. Then one day you have to face the fact it's not here any more.

For Rosalind, also in her mid-50s, the menopause brought up the grief of never having conceived. She and her husband had spent years going to fertility clinics.

> I started the menopause early – I must have been around 40, and I remember thinking, 'This is it.' The opportunity had gone. I knew I didn't want to continue to try either. In a way it was a relief because there was no longer any hope. It was like getting life back onto an even keel, making the most of what I had and realizing life still held a lot of meaning without having children.

We're going to move away from sexual identity and fertility issues to hear about other challenges and experiences that interviewees wanted to talk about. There are more of course, than those given, but I hope the examples illustrate how complex and challenging this stage of life can be, and how poorly recognized it is by society.

The sandwich generation

Several women talked with me about what it's like to be part of what is called the 'sandwich generation'. Fifty-nine-year-old Maureen spoke of how she had looked forward to having time with her husband after their three children had left home. But freedom to do what they wanted didn't last long. Maureen's daughter became pregnant, and her mother developed Alzheimer's. As her daughter had to work full-time in order to meet mortgage payments, Maureen now spent most of her time either helping to look after her grandchild or visiting her mother in a care home. She told me,

> I don't want to sound bitter about my life. I love my grandchild and I want to visit my mother regularly. But I often wonder if I've missed the boat. I mean, when will it be my turn to enjoy myself, and for us as a couple to do all the travelling that we've dreamed of for so long.

Maureen is not alone. One in eight adults now has elderly parents or in-laws who need assistance. During 2010 alone, it is estimated that these elderly parents in the UK will receive around £21 billion worth of unpaid care and help from their adult children, many of whom are of course also caring for their own families.

Older single mum

I spoke to several women about the challenges of being older mothers to young children. However, I was deeply moved when 57-year-old Lindsey told me what it was like to care for elderly parents at the same time as being a single mother to a nine-year-old. After a serious accident in her early teens she was told by doctors she couldn't have children. She never married, but at the age of 48 she fell pregnant. It was, to put it mildly, a shock, especially when her boyfriend ended the relationship and had never contributed financially to their son's upkeep.

> Most people think I did it deliberately – which I certainly didn't – and I know several doctors believe my son's an IVF baby, which he most certainly is not. I would never dream of saying he's a mistake. Unplanned, yes. But when I fell pregnant I knew I really, really wanted the baby.
> Even so, it's the isolation I find difficult. I don't know of anyone else in the same situation. I've not just got very different values from younger mothers, I'm also standing at the school gate having hot flushes. In addition, he's only got my parents as grandparents, but really they should be his great-grandparents. They're very frail these days, and I feel increasingly responsible for them too.

It's been incredibly hard work bringing my son up on my own. I've had to sacrifice so much to make sure he has what he needs. There's nothing left over for me, and now he's nine, I'm beginning to notice he doesn't want to be around me so much. It's hard to accept, but that's what happens.

By the time he leaves home I'll be in my late 60s, and most of my life will be over. But I've accepted that I had my life before I had him, and I don't expect anything else now, apart to continue to care for my parents. As long as I can get into the fresh air every day, I'm okay, and I take great solace from my garden.

Even though I look at my son as my miracle, I am aware that older women who get pregnant deliberately, for example, through IVF treatment, usually have family support and financial stability. I would *never* recommend that a woman on her own in her late 40s does this, no matter how desperate she is to have a baby.

Living alone

A number of divorced and single women I spoke to told me how hard it was to accept that they couldn't find new partners.

Jane, a divorced mother of two children no longer at home, described the grief of facing the future as a single woman still only in her 50s.

I find it immensely challenging. The dream I was sold as a young woman of growing old with the partner I married never happened to me. He left me to bring up my children alone. Now I am postmenopausal, I have to face the fact that part of me has died, but I still feel that I have so much living to do. It's hard, because I don't want to do things on my own all the time.

However, I'm learning to accept that I can't expect someone else to make me happy. I'm beginning to come out the other side knowing that if I don't meet someone it will be okay. It has to be.

Candice is in her late 50s. She, too, is divorced.

I'm learning to accept what happens in the moment. But that doesn't diminish how much I would love to share my life with someone – to find someone to grow old with. It doesn't seem fair that I frittered away my youth doing daft things with emotionally immature men because I didn't know how to handle myself differently. Now I'm older and wiser, and would make a far better partner, men of my age don't seem to be interested. I find that really painful.

'It's really difficult to meet men of your own age,' agreed 56-year-old Diana. She had started using internet dating websites. In her case, it hadn't been a success.

> I was searching for a serious, meaningful partner who had integrity. I had hundreds of responses, and whittled them down to three dates. First one seemed to go well but I never heard from him again. Second one had sexual hang-ups, and I didn't like the third one at all. They were all in their mid to late 50s. Right age group, but none of them were interested in a menopausal woman. I am sure they were looking for a woman who could give them a second family.

Linda, a widow in her early 60s, hadn't had much luck with internet dating either.

> It was devastating when my husband died. I was just coming up to 60. I don't know how I managed to get through that first year. We always had a good sex life, and I miss it dreadfully. I do lots of things with my life, but it's difficult to meet men at my age. I did meet someone through an internet dating site. He was very good in bed but I knew he wasn't right for me. I haven't given up though. I don't do internet dating any more, but I keep an eye out. You never know.

I love Linda's positive attitude, and it's important to realize that romance isn't just for the young. Internet dating may not work for some, but for others it does. I know of three couples in their 50s and 60s who have met like this. Others I know have met through the Friends Reunited website, and there's a new site called *Friends over Fifty* that caters for older people seeking partners. At the time of writing, nearly three million men and women have registered.

Much happier alone

In complete contrast, for other women the thought of finding a new partner doesn't appeal at all. Sixty-seven-year-old Clare was delighted to be living on her own.

I am a widow and I haven't had a sexual partner for almost ten years. I don't miss it at all. I like my independence, and anyway, I don't have time for it.

I never intended to go into another relationship when I split up from my first husband. I met my second husband shortly after the divorce, but he died of cancer a few years later.

Life has taught me you never know what's around the corner. Even so, it would be a miracle if I met someone who I wanted to be with these days. I have no desire to go through the rigmarole of another relationship. Anyway, relationships take up too much time. I still teach part-time. Two nights a week I play in a samba band, and every Wednesday night I go out with colleagues for a walk and a meal. I love studying too. I've just finished an Open University degree and I'm thinking of doing another one as well.

One or two friends are in a relationship and one would like to be married because she's never had the experience. But the rest of my friends are single, widowed or divorced and they feel the same as me. Relationships are a lot of work.

Clare's attitude is not unusual. A 2008 report by the Economic and Social Research Council found that women over 60 who live alone are happier and healthier than when they live with husbands and partners. (For men, incidentally, it's the other way round. They do much better when partnered.) Similar to Clare, many single older women form close friendships, have busy and fulfilling lives, and even when they are in a relationship, they seldom want to give up their independent lifestyles. I have to say, I wouldn't rush into another relationship if anything were to happen to my husband. I love sharing our lives together, and thoroughly enjoy the relationship I have built with my step-children, but at this stage of my life, I wouldn't want to take on someone else – or their children and grandchildren. And, let's be honest, men need a lot of looking after.

Nevertheless, in direct contrast to the report above which says that women can be happier on their own, a 2008 study from the Institute of Public Policy Research is concerned about the rising numbers of lonely and depressed older women living alone. So, whatever your circumstances, it's important to have a good network of friends, and to get out and about.

Credibility in the workplace

There are still huge imbalances in the representation of women in higher levels of commerce, politics and management. But since women's lib and the social changes of the 1960s and 70s, women of the baby boomer generation have undoubtedly found a voice and a respect in the business community that wasn't there before. One might imagine that these mature women are now at the height of their careers and mentoring those coming up the ladder. However, according to several interviewees, this isn't necessarily so.

So, we're going to finish the chapter with hearing what it's like for working women to go through the menopause. For some, this was a very painful and contentious issue. For others, the menopause coincided with a feeling of at last hitting their stride. Finally, we hear from an interviewee who provided a seldom-heard view of what it's like to age in the sex industry itself.

We'll start with those who are finding the workplace increasingly difficult, such as 59-year-old Rosemary. She is a freelance market researcher employed by one company for several years. Her job involves a good deal of direct contact with the public. Although official and acceptable retirement age in the UK is already 65, and set to rise further, and despite new legislation outlawing age discrimination, Rosemary told me she was terrified her bosses would find out she was approaching 60.

'They might not want me any more,' she said. 'But then again, I must being doing quite a good job at what I do because they know my daughter is in her 30s. I really like my job, but I am getting increasingly anxious about whether I am going to be sidelined when my contract comes up for renewal.'

Judith, a 58-year-old director of a company linked to the advertising industry, believed she was also facing a new form of ageism and sexism now she was an older woman.

> I set up the company with a female colleague in the 1980s. We were regarded as pioneers in those days and we attracted a lot of attention. Part of it was about being good-looking women; part of it was to do with the superwoman thing. We were working mothers building successful careers.
>
> That's changed. The company is no longer functioning at the same level. It could be the market, but the fact of being an older woman in a business that's notoriously youth orientated is not easy. Older men

are seen differently. You just have to look at ageing male rock stars who get away with it. You never see ageing female rock stars do the same thing. The over-sexualization of young women by the media doesn't help either because older women can't play those cards any more.

I asked Judith how the menopause has affected her personally.

I am much more anxious than I used to be. I get worked up about timings, travel arrangements, and trying to remember things. I've also become much more nervous when I speak publicly, something I used to just accept. It's a shock because I always imagined things kept on getting better after you've been doing it for years.

Christine, another successful businesswoman in her mid-50s, had also experienced loss of confidence since the menopause.

I think I'm less authoritative, and I question myself much more. You don't have time to do this when you're younger. Your energy levels are different, and you just get on with it.

I work in the commercial world, developing change programmes for corporate companies. It's a young person's area, and I am very aware that I am changing into the elder stateswoman. Younger clients are okay with me chairing committees, but they don't want to commission projects from their mother. That's a hard fact to take on board, but it's increasingly evident. The other day I was at a conference talking to a much younger woman. I said something to her and she looked at me as if to say, but I wasn't even born then!

I asked Christine how she saw her future. She was distressed about the changes that she faced.

I'm reaching a point where I need to think of doing something else. But this is a hard transition to go through because I've been on top of my profession for over 30 years. It's nothing to do with money, it's about being forced to redefine myself when I don't want to, and to ask the question, who am I without my job? It's causing me a lot of anxiety and sleepless nights. I don't want to end up volunteering for charitable organizations. A lot of friends of similar age are doing that, but I think I'm worth more than accepting that I have to fade away. Men don't take on these non-paid jobs like women do.

Claire, the 67-year-old teacher we met earlier, also experienced a combination of sexism and ageism.

> I've always enjoyed working and still do, but it's not great being an older woman in my job. I come across a lot of men from the Middle East in the classroom who are flabbergasted that I am still at it. 'Why aren't your children looking after you?' they keep asking. I also lose out to male colleagues. I enjoy teaching business studies but they get those jobs.

Kathy, another of my Sex, Meaning and Menopause workshop participants, complained about the lack of respect she received, despite being highly experienced in her field of work.

> I've been working as an aromatherapist for 20 years and I am still treated like a newcomer. I've decided to pull out of my professional body because of it. There's no facility for mentoring new people coming into the business, or even accepting you have anything worthwhile to offer, even though you've been at it for years. I know this doesn't just happen in my avenue of work, but I think it's sad how little recognition is given to older people – whether you are male or female – or that our life experience isn't recognized in financial terms. It's all about cost-cutting and employing newly qualified people because they are cheaper – and probably don't answer back.

I want to add a comment from Kathryn Colas, who runs the Simply Hormones website, an excellent resource on the menopause which includes information for working women. She travels the country running workshops to educate human resource managers and directors on the menopause and how it can affect work performance.

> Women are often too embarrassed to talk about what's really wrong. They don't want to talk to their managers either, and senior female executives are also having similar issues. They are frightened of being marginalized, and some even leave their job because they feel they've lost control over their body. Apart from the embarrassment of hot flushes, a big issue is often weight gain. This is perfectly natural during the menopause, but who warns you about it? You end up going mad on diets, but your metabolism has changed. It causes a lot of distress.

I see these young female human resource directors thinking, 'Gosh, this is going to happen to me too one day.' Men make a joke of it, but they haven't got a clue what's happening.

There are several other very good websites, such as Menopause Support, set up by Heather Fairbairn and her husband as a not-for-profit social enterprise. Their aim is to raise awareness on different aspects of the menopause and to run a Menopause Support Programme. Contact details can be found in the Helpful websites section at the end of this book.

Hitting their stride

Academics and those who worked in areas where men and women were regarded as equal appeared to have a much better time than those in the business sector. For example, 55-year-old Caroline is a university professor.

Getting older has no effect on how my peers perceive me. In fact it's an asset. I am now in a position where I mentor younger people. I get a tremendous amount from that, and also from the respect I receive as someone who's gained the level of expertise that I have.

Nevertheless, outside her working environment, Caroline realized she is now an invisible menopausal woman.

Of course, if you saw me in the street you wouldn't know me from a glass of water, but that doesn't matter to me. I'm fulfilled from the inside, and I am fortunate enough to have friends and family who support and validate me on a personal level. But, without that support I know I would find it difficult.

Fifty-four-year-old Marianne had also had positive experiences. She works with environmental issues.

My work has really taken off and it forms the central meaning to my life. I've at last found how to weave together all the things I have done in the past. Talking as a menopausal woman, I suppose you could say I am weaving my cloth. It's a very good feeling.

It's also scary because I have to do a lot of public speaking, and it's strange to find myself in this position. In the past, I've tended to be the youngest in group settings. Now I see myself as the older wise woman, with younger people looking up to me in the same way I used to look up to group leaders.

However, Marianne struggles with how younger people react to her.

I'm conscious that young men look through me these days. I've noticed that with my children. I am interested to hear what their friends have to say, but it's obvious by the look on their faces that I don't interest them at all. I find that very odd.

Ageing in the sex industry

Coping with the menopause is clearly more stressful for some working women than others, but listening to their stories made me think about what happens when a woman ages in the world's oldest profession.

Sandra is a 60-year-old ex-prostitute. She turned to sex work in her early 40s when she ran short of money, and found it a relatively easy way to make a living. She only worked in safe environments – never on the street – and was always in full control of who she saw as clients. However, she realized that as she approached her 50s her days were numbered.

You know you're up against it, but as long as you can land a trick, you keep going.

I have no idea if many older sex workers use HRT. I've never discussed it with anyone. But a lot use Botox and have cosmetic help. You have to keep your face, tits and bum together if you want to carry on, and keeping up your appearance can be bloody hard work.

Personally, I had a straightforward menopause. I'd been working for about 15 years by then. I had a good body, auburn hair and green eyes, and I always looked younger that I was. But I knew that a day would come when someone would say, 'No thanks.'

Exactly that happened. I was working as an escort at the time. I arrived at the hotel room and a young man opened the door. He took one look at me and said, 'I don't want to have sex with someone of my mother's age.' I was fed up because I thought I had made it clear on the telephone that I was older. He had poor English, so perhaps he hadn't understood. But, I was also furious. I had spent a lot of time getting myself together – you have to because everything's different. Thinning pubic hair is just one example. Older women from all over the world have to face this if they are sex workers.

I stopped doing it regularly when I was in my mid-50s, although I did continue to see a few clients, older men who I knew. They would have liked to have carried on, but I decided at a certain point I had had enough. However, I do know older prostitutes who continue. They often form private cooperatives together so they can look out for each other. But I'm glad I don't have to work any more. I am more financially stable, and quite honestly I can't be bothered with it all. I would much rather have a cup of tea.

As myths go, talking to an older woman who'd worked in the sex trade was about as busting an experience as I could have imagined. By the end of the interview, I certainly liked and greatly respected Sandra. I also thoroughly enjoyed the humour we shared as we got our spectacles out to read the menu, and knew we'd both rather have a cuppa than a romp between the sheets.

So, onwards with how the mechanics of sex changes during the menopause.

CHAPTER 3

Menopausal mechanics of sex

One of the biggest issues for those I interviewed was the mechanics of what happens to sex during the menopause. It's a far more complex – and thorny – problem than just being a sexual dysfunction that needs fixing. So, this chapter looks at the range of sexual changes that can happen (and the effects this has on relationships), the sexual differences between older men and women, and at how, sometimes with a helping hand from HRT, a new breed of sexually liberated postmenopausal women are thoroughly enjoying themselves.

Talking about sex

I appreciate that talking about sex and the menopause can be tricky. Embarking on the task, I certainly feel a bit wobbly atop my soapbox. Mind you, being brought up by a generation that regarded menstruation as 'the curse', it's small wonder we baby boomers continue to struggle to find the language or the space to address such a taboo subject.

Fifty-five-year-old Bettina put it this way:

> What happens at the menopause is such an unknown quantity. Society prepares you for childhood, adolescence, even the midlife crisis. But there's nothing about what happens in your 50s and how the menopause changes everything. It's like living on a blank page, especially when it comes to sex.

A few of the married women I spoke to were happy to talk to friends, and sometimes to partners, about the sexual changes they were going through. However, the vast majority said they rarely, if ever, talked about what was happening to them. Most said they had learned about sexual changes 'as they went along'. Several women said they found it hard to find other women to talk to about it. One woman said, 'There seems to be a general reticence to admit to anything to do with menopause apart from having the odd hot flush.'

Mothers hadn't been much help either. Several women spoke of the 'wall of silence' from their parents around anything to do with sex. One workshop participant said that the only advice her mother had given her when she started her period was that hair would start to grow under her armpits. She knew then that she would never be able to ask her mother for advice about anything that really mattered, and certainly not the menopause.

In fact, 53-year-old Heather said that talking to me about sex at this time of life made her feel like a pioneer, because so few people she knew spoke about it in any depth. Sally, a 56-year-old businesswoman, had no idea what other women of the same age were experiencing sexually. She didn't like to ask. 'It's strange considering we talk about everything else,' she said, adding that she had been shocked when a friend had dropped into the conversation that she didn't want sex any more. 'I felt too uncomfortable to ask her about it.'

Nina, a television producer in her mid-50s, had never told anyone about the difficulties loss of sexual desire was causing in her relationship. 'There's an assumption that 'we're meant to get on with it. Perhaps it's down to the British stiff-upper-lip thing.' Sixty-two-year-old Patti never told anyone how painful sex had become for her. 'Am I abnormal?' she asked. She had no idea, and had kept silent because she didn't want to betray her husband by admitting they no longer had such a satisfying sex life.

Some women had never even spoken to a doctor about what was happening to them. Kerstin is in her mid-50s. 'I've got a basic understanding of the biological and hormonal changes that are happening to me,' she told me, 'but I've never spoken to anyone medical about it.'

The more I listened to these women, the sadder I felt about the way sex and the menopause have become, as it were, the elephant in the room, especially when we women have so little difficulty talking about almost anything and everything else.

The taboo of sex and the menopause

So, this is a good moment to consider why talking about sex and the menopause is such a taboo. To do this, we need to step back in time.

Until the industrial revolution, and the advent of health care, most of us in the West wouldn't have had to think about sex as older women. Either we would have died in childbirth, or we would have been wiped out by illness or disease before we reached it.

More recently, the First and Second World Wars left hundreds of thousands of women single, either as widows who never married again, or as spinsters who remained unwed quite simply because there were not enough men to go round. And of course, society was very different. There were much stricter religious and moral codes of ethics, especially around sex, and it just 'wasn't done' to talk about such things. I remember my grandmother would only refer to 'things below the waist'. My mother wasn't that much better.

This all changed on 23 June 1960 when the US Food and Drugs Administration approved the world's first birth control pill, and for the first time in history, gave women almost full personal control over their fertility.

By the time I arrived in London in 1971 to train as a nurse, sexual liberation was in full swing. During my first week at my teaching hospital, which was located just around the corner from Carnaby Street (the reason why I chose to train there), I vividly recall a sturdy-legged tutor strongly recommending a visit to our hospital GP to 'sort ourselves out'. It was expected that we would be sexually active, and The Pill – so powerful was its impact that it needed no other introduction – became the accepted damage-control method for all of us who were unmarried. There was a new openness about contraception and sex. Previously, I remember the embarrassment of finding a Dutch Cap in my mother's underwear drawer and asking what it was. Now there were IUDs (intrauterine devices) and of course, condoms (I remember them also being called Johnnies or rubbers). As well as being available in those much sniggered-over Packs-of-Three from the chemist, or slipped into the back pocket after the barber enquired whether 'Sir' might require anything for the weekend, we and our boyfriends could now buy condoms from public vending machines in railway stations, lavatories and clubs.

We had the protection against pregnancy and encouragement to enjoy sex for its own sake – but I wonder how many of us really did. Few of us, I suspect, had the emotional intelligence to understand the difference between making love and having sex, and many of my generation ended up in one kind of emotional mess or another because of it. This hasn't stopped. We, the baby boomer generation, seem to have embraced divorce as if it were a lifestyle choice.

Emotional messes or not, vast improvements in medical treatment since the 1960s mean that those of us reaching menopause today can expect to have a good one-third of our lives left to live – and to continue, if we wish, to be as sexually liberated as we were as young women. But that's an expectation which comes with a whole new set of emotional stresses for us to cope with.

As Professor Lorraine Dennerstein from Melbourne University put it to me, 'the problem is down to Mother Nature'.

> Sex is really about the continuation of the species, but we've progressed far beyond this hunter–gatherer mentality. The trouble is, our biology hasn't kept up with it.
>
> In simplistic terms, men and women originally had sex to procreate. Fertile women had to want sex in order for this to happen. However, lots of women died in childbirth, so the man would find another mate, and so on. Those women who survived childbirth died around the menopause. Any who made it into older age helped to care for the young, and died soon after.

Reflecting on how my early ancestors experienced sex, I was reminded of a wonderful BBC wildlife documentary from Central Africa which introduced us to two female mountain gorillas at different ends of the fertility scale. A glossy, doe-eyed pubescent gorilla – equivalent human age probably mid to late teens – was shown throwing herself at any male she could find, whether young male blackback (which caused ructions when the leading silverback discovered them at it) or the silverback himself. Although willing to mate, the older gorilla clearly found the youngster immature and irritating – much as many older, mature men might judge the very similar antics of bare-midriffed, hopelessly high-heeled, shrieking, male-attention-seeking teenaged girls who throng our town and city streets on Friday and Saturday nights.

At the other end of the scale, the film told the story of an older female, 35 in gorilla years and probably mid-60s in human terms, who was clearly and very, very firmly in the not-interested-in-sex, postmenopausal camp. She treated her group's sexually bothersome silverback leader with such disdain and contempt that I felt almost as sorry for him as I do sometimes for my own silverback at home. We are, in other words, but primates, with our evolutionary conditioning still firmly in place.

Back to our modern, human experience. Today, the average life expectancy for a woman in the UK is an astounding mid-80s, and the upper 70s for men, decades longer than we could have expected only a hundred years ago. However, the average age for a woman to start going through the menopause hasn't changed. It remains at just past 50. The shocking reality – unimaginable to most younger women I've talked with about this – is that our female experience of sex, so central to the first 40-odd years of our adulthood, radically changes when we still have the prospect of another three or four decades to live.

Not only are we women forced to redefine our relationship with our bodies, and with sex and physical intimacy, but it's a change that confronts our relationships with the reality that sex may never again be as satisfying as it was, or indeed possible again at all. No wonder this is such a critical time in a marriage, and I am alarmed how little this is talked about, either publicly or, as it became clear to me researching this book, privately between couples.

I asked Wendy Maltz, an American sex therapist, what we can realistically expect sexually as we reach the menopause. All of us, she told me, both men and women, will have to face the reality that sexual experiences can be less frequent and powerful as we grow older.

> It's part of the natural changes that take place. We become less intensely driven, because we don't have as many sex hormones cheering us on from the sidelines. Staying sexually active in midlife is about staying physically fit and figuring out a way to keep inspiration alive. It's not a good idea to strive hard to meet some imagined goal and force things. Sex may not work 100 per cent every time, so it's about being flexible and creative. Sometimes, you might need to throw in the towel and have a cup of tea instead. Couples who do well learn to accept that when their hearts are in the right place, whatever they do together is good enough.

I think it's important to mention that, in this context, Wendy is referring to sex involving penetration. In fact, *The Handbook of Sexuality in Close Relationships*, produced in the US, reports that most people associate having sex with full sexual intercourse. Remember Bill Clinton's famous remark about his liaison with the young White House intern Monica Lewinsky in the mid-1990s: 'I did not have sexual relations with that woman.' Certainly when I was young, oral sex and sexual foreplay was not considered 'going all the way'. And, of course, as Bill Clinton knows, there are many ways to enjoy sexual intimacy without penetration. For example, there's oral sex, stroking genitals, firing each other up on the telephone (Prince Charles and Camilla come to mind), 'sexting' – sending sex messages by text – or even just lying together skin-on-skin, as we will hear in Chapter 5 from one man I interviewed. Nevertheless, most women I interviewed talked about penetrative sex, because this was causing the most problems in their relationship.

Mechanical changes in sex

Talking to interviewees, it seemed to me that how women experience the shifting mechanics of sex during and after the menopause falls loosely (very loosely) into six categories. At its most uninhibited, some women undergo a surge in sexual feelings. Others, on the whole, continue enjoying sex much as before. A third group experience a general lessening in sexual desire. A fourth group, who may still in theory like the idea, experience a sudden and dramatic death of libido. A fifth group, quite a large one I discovered, found sex horribly painful. Then there's the sixth group who were actually relieved it was all over.

Putting aside other health issues, it's important to stress that all these categories are *normal* sexual responses to what happens when the menopause arrives. How you deal with the impact this may have on your life or on your relationship is another matter. These days we have a choice. For instance, some women take different forms of HRT to continue an active sex life (we'll be looking at the pros and cons of HRT in Chapter 6). Others wouldn't dream of using artificial hormones, even if this ultimately means the death of their libido.

But, let's start with the first category.

1. A surge in sexual feelings

Although none of my interviewees said they had experienced this, it's important to allow that during the menopause, some women do undoubtedly have a surge in sexual energy – indeed, sometimes embarrassingly and inappropriately so. This is caused when the ovaries continue to produce significant amounts of testosterone (which isn't just a male sex hormone, women produce it too), even though progesterone and oestrogen levels are falling. The consequence can be a rush of sexual desire, at least for a time. One of my interviewees told me that it happened to a friend of hers who initially enjoyed her new-found sexual energy. But it wasn't all positive, as this friend found herself getting into a number of unwelcome and embarrassing scrapes with people she would never have normally found attractive. Fortunately (or perhaps not), she was already divorced by this time.

2. Still enjoying sex

Several women I spoke to hadn't experienced any sexual changes at all. Carmen, 63 and very much through the menopause, couldn't imagine a time when she won't have sex. 'We've been through the parenting thing,' she said, 'and are now into this period of our lives when we are much freer, and have a lot more privacy.' Janet is 55, and she told me that both her children had left home. That meant that she and her new partner, with whom she now lives, now had time to enjoy a very sexual relationship.

> My previous husband became impotent when I was 40, and I didn't have sex for a long time. It was a joy to discover it again with my new partner. We have a fabulous sex life. My only issue is that I've become a lot drier and have to use lubricants, but it's not a problem for either of us. So, I look at sex as the one area where I can celebrate becoming an older woman. I have much more time and space to indulge in it – no children barging in, or fear of pregnancy. No pills or devices, and much more awareness of my needs and how my body works.

Diana, in her 60s, was also enjoying a vibrant sex life. 'I used to be in a very destructive relationship so I know about not wanting sex. But now I'm in a new relationship, my sex drive has shot up again.' Another woman looked aghast that I should even ask her the question, saying 'Of course I still have sex. The menopause has made no difference at all.'

For 56-year-old Maureen, it's more complicated. Maureen has been married for over 30 years, and has three children. She told me that she continued to want sex, but she and her husband no longer had a sexual relationship. So, to meet her sexual needs she got together with a couple every few months, as a threesome. The arrangement had been going on for over five years.

Sex gives me fulfilment. It's warm, loving, exciting, vibrant, and makes me tingle. I'm not prepared to give it up because it would mean losing part of myself.

I don't want a full-on affair. It's too dangerous. I come from a broken home so I would never put my children through that – which is why this arrangement works well. I would love to see the couple more than I do, but we have to tiptoe around my husband. Originally we used to swap as two couples, but the two men didn't get on so that particular arrangement had to stop. I've carried on seeing the couple, but I haven't told my husband. I don't want to push it into his face. If he did know, he might get a bit funny – I wouldn't like that. But if he doesn't want to make love to me, what am I to do?

For some women without partners or lovers, the desire to have sex was causing them considerable distress. Anna's husband died a couple of years ago. She is now in her mid-60s.

We had a wonderful sex life all the way through our marriage. Of course I miss him dreadfully, but I also miss sex like mad. At times it's quite uncomfortable. I've had a couple of lovers, but they haven't worked out. One particularly was great in bed, but pretty useless otherwise. At my age, it's very hard to find someone who is sexually and emotionally compatible. I try to put my sexual energy into other things I enjoy, but it's not easy, and most people would be horrified if they knew how much I still miss it.

Other women talked of their continued enjoyment of sex, but admitted it wasn't as frequent as it used to be. At the age of 61, Penny was still very much enjoying a good sex life, although she noticed a change in her libido. She'd been married to her second husband for almost 25 years. 'We do it at least twice a week. I'm not as desperate for it as I used to be, but I believe it releases oxytocins that make you feel good, and it certainly brings us closer together.'

Sarah had also noticed a difference in her sex drive since she went through an early menopause at the age of 43. Married now for more than 40 years, she and her husband still have regular sex, at least twice a week. 'It used to be four times,' she told me, 'but your libido does change.' Sarah says she finds sex much nicer these days. 'When you're younger, you worry about if you're doing it right. Now it's just comfortable.' She can't imagine a time when she and her husband won't be having sex, and finds it hard to imagine any woman not wanting to continue enjoying sex, considering the strains that might place on relationships.

It was refreshing to hear that sex can be enjoyed during and after the menopause. But many of the women I spoke to were struggling with fading or now non-existent libidos. Some had thought of using HRT, but decided against it either for general health reasons or, like me, because there was no way they would use artificial hormones.

3. Losing interest

Before we go into the detail of this middle group of women, still capable of having sex but not really bothered any more, or who have sex only to keep their partners happy, it's worth considering what scientific research rather than just anecdotal evidence tells us of women's changing interest in sex as they reach the change of life.

In Australia in 2005, Professor Lorraine Dennerstein led a study to explore the actual experience of 450 women as they approached and then went through the menopause.

When first interviewed, a (to me) surprisingly high number of the participants, 40 per cent, already reported what would be clinically described as sexual dysfunction; that is, problems with sex to the point of needing treatment. What's even more telling is that, by the time the whole group of women had gone through the menopause, 80 per cent – yes, well over three-quarters of them – could be considered as having a similar level of sexual dysfunction.

And now the rub. Just 17 per cent of the entire now postmenopausal group – that's fewer than one in five – were distressed by these sexual changes. In fact, some told their interviewers that they found it a good excuse to give up sex altogether, especially if they were in a poor relationship.

In contrast, women who had been sexually active *and* in good relationships were more likely to be upset by the loss of libido. These women wanted to continue the same level of intimacy with their partners, but were finding it difficult or impossible. Women who were depressed were also more likely to be negatively affected, as an expression of their overall low self-esteem issues.

The study concluded that women who do wish to consider treatment for sexual dysfunction during the menopause should be offered support based on a comprehensive psychological and physiological evaluation. In other words, they should be offered a good deal more than just treatment with drugs. The survey results also reinforced the importance of open, honest communication between couples if they wish to continue a good relationship, especially when there is a drop in libido.

So, back to our own interviewees in this third, 'losing interest' category.

'I don't think having grown-up children helps,' said one woman. 'I hadn't anticipated how this can desexualize you. I'm not one to live vicariously through my kids, but there is a degree to which you start feeling like an old piece of furniture.' Another woman approaching 50, who had always practised the rhythm method as contraception, said she put her fading interest in sex down to the fear of getting pregnant. 'My periods are all over the place these days. So I can't trust what's happening in my body any more. But, I admit it's easy to come up with excuses, and you can get out of practice.'

Margie, a 55-year-old fashion designer, was struggling to find the middle ground between her own dwindling desire for sex and her husband's, which hadn't changed. Although distressed by these changes, she certainly did not describe herself as having a 'malfunction'. She told me, 'It's just what's happening, as it does to most women of my age'.

> But it seems difficult for my husband to understand what I'm going through. We have sex once or twice a week these days. I would prefer once a fortnight, but I never get to the point of wanting it anyway. So we've learnt to compromise between what my husband wants and what I want. He thinks it's slightly too little, I think it's slightly too much.
>
> It does piss me off at times, because I would rather go to sleep. But I don't feel annoyed with him. In fact I feel envious that he still wants it. I don't like this feeling of being depleted of sexual desire, and it's very different when you're not sexually active in your head any more either. It makes me sad. I'm missing a part of me who was a very sexy person.

Lesley, who has been married to her husband for over 35 years, was saddened that neither she nor her husband had the same level of interest in sex any more.

> We've always enjoyed making love to each other. On Saturday nights, if we weren't doing anything else, I'd put on sexy underwear under

my clothes. We'd have dinner and then have sex right afterwards on the floor. It was a great occasion for us both. We still do our Saturday night thing, but not as much. It does bother me sometimes, but I can't pretend it's that same driving passion and excitement these days. It's more of a comfortable feeling – an extension of a warm cuddle in the morning.

Sometimes I ask my husband why we don't have as much sex as we used to. He says his sex drive isn't as strong as it was either. I suppose we do it every two-to-three weeks. I wonder if that's normal for people in their 60s.

I was taken aback by Lesley's wondering whether having sex every two or three weeks was normal for a couple of her age. Of course it is. In fact in my experience of writing this book, that's quite a lot for some couples, but Lesley's question does illustrate how little sex is spoken about in later life.

Although a survey conducted by the condom manufacturer Durex in 2003 said sex two or three times a week is the 'norm' for couples living together, I am wary of reducing lovemaking to a set of homogenized statistics. The frequency and quality of sex depends on health, state of mind, quality of relationship and, of course, phase of life.

It also depends on sexual expectations. These can be high when we're at that same sexually excitable stage as our young pubescent female gorilla – especially when it comes to the humble orgasm. But, similar to the gorilla matriarch sitting at the other end of the scale, things tend to cool down as we go through the menopause.

Victoria, a 58-year-old university lecturer, said she accepted that she no longer had orgasms, and looked at it as part of her natural ageing process.

We still have sex, but these days I never reach a climax. My husband is the same age, and he's getting older as well. It's not as if he's a young virile man and I'm the only one who's ageing. We're both doing this together.

However, 62-year-old Nicola has found the loss far more distressing. Reaching orgasm had always played a major part in her enjoyment of sex.

That physical ache that gets satisfied by orgasm has gone. I used to love sex. Really love it. I used to plan for it. Now it represents something different. Sometimes I just endure it, and sometimes I share it.

I've never told my partner how I feel because I still find the closeness of an intimate relationship comforting. I don't think he guesses what I am going through. I admit I am duplicitous with him. I pretend I'm enjoying sex more than I do. But then I'm not going to let him bang up and down on top of me and tell him I'm bored, am I?!

Nicola is not alone in how she hides the truth from her partner. Many women I spoke to confessed that they only have penetrative sex for their partner's sake.

'I have sex because I feel it should be part of our relationship,' admitted one woman. She added,

I never expected to lose the urge like this. It's caused a lot of complications with my partner, so I try to comply as much as I can. I suppose we do it about once a week these days.

Once a week?! That sounds pretty active to me, but, as we noted earlier, everyone's expectations are particular to them. Another woman, a retired dance teacher who had just turned 60, also admitted to similar motivations for sex.

I wouldn't do it if I didn't think my husband was so special. He's very open, and has encouraged me to find ways that help me to enjoy sex. But I know I've changed in that department. When he's not around I seldom think about sex, and it wouldn't really bother me if I never had it again. But it is difficult when you're in a relationship.

She then acknowledged an underlying fear:

Men are different to women. They don't necessarily want to leave their wives, but they can easily be waylaid by a younger woman. They may have a good relationship, a nice home and grandchildren whizzing about, but something is lacking for them. There are lots of women out there who are lonely and who would love to be with a guy. The thing is to stay on your toes. I take care of myself, and I never take my husband for granted. I will have sex for as long as he wants to.

I particularly enjoyed a wry comment made by Wendy, a teacher in her mid-60s when we were having a cup of coffee together. She has been married to her second (much younger) husband for 15 years.

> Yes, you do dry out as you grow older, but you have to make an effort. I spent 30 years grumbling about how rotten my sex life was with my first husband. I remarried when I was 50, so I can hardly start complaining about it again, can I?

Well, yes you could, but similar to Wendy, many women continue to have sex even though they're not that interested any more.

4. 'Sudden death'

In France, they call the orgasm 'le petit mort' – the small death. For some women, however, the menopause can be a very big death, finding them completely unprepared for how rapidly sexual changes can happen. That's what happened to me, so I particularly empathized with Belinda, who said it felt as if part of her had died, literally overnight. 'One day,' she told me, 'I just didn't want to have sex. It was as simple as that.'

Belinda has been with her partner for almost 15 years, but her abrupt sexual change was putting their relationship under considerable strain.

> It's very distressing because my partner can't understand what's going on. It's made me feel as if there was something wrong with me. That I am failing him. But if you don't want sex, what do you do? Pretend?
>
> It's not just that I don't want to have sex; I don't want to be sexually touched at all. It's certainly put a strain on our relationship to the point that I'm not sure I want to go on with it. I hate feeling sexually pressurized by him all the time.

I think Belinda named a hugely important issue, which I have also had to confront in my own relationship. When sex is an accepted part of a healthy relationship, it rarely needs to be discussed. However, when it suddenly stops, the absence of sex can become a looming, negative presence for the two of you. To work it out together needs a great deal of patience as well as an understanding partner. Or this can be a time to reassess what you both really want.

For Nina, the 55-year-old television producer, the death of sexual desire had brought some painful realizations to the surface.

> I was sexually abused as a child, so I never really understood boundaries. I spent years confusing sex with love, and it was only when I met my partner that love and sex came together comfortably. We had a relatively good sex life until I reached around 50. Then almost from one day to the next, my desire turned off. Last year we probably made love five times.
>
> It has put considerable strain on our relationship, but maybe I just don't fancy him any more. I've never admitted to this before, but I do wonder if it would make a difference if I met someone who turned me on again.

Some women's sex drives had been dramatically affected by medication taken, for example, after breast cancer treatment. Susanne was entirely unprepared for the way it affected her libido, and said it had added to the distress of what she had already gone through.

> In spite of my marriage being difficult for many years, we've always had a good sex life. But the death of my sex drive makes me feel like a failure. I keep thinking I should be working on having sex. Then I think, what's the point if I have no longing for it. Then I think, why am I bothering to look attractive anyway? And I beat myself up for sending out the wrong signals to my husband. At the same time I can't believe I will never feel sexual again, so it's very confusing.

Elspeth, whose sexual desire also died after treatment for breast cancer, never imagined this could happen to her. She told me, 'I'm not ready for it. I don't want to be like this. It makes me resentful and I also feel like a failure.' That word failure again.

Elspeth had found it particularly difficult to come to terms with the loss of her libido, because she believed sex contributed to her healing.

> Sex for me has always been important. A lifesaver, even. When I was having chemotherapy for breast cancer we would have sex before the treatments. My white blood cell count would always be up when they tested my blood, so I knew it boosted my immune system.
>
> I miss feeling that intimacy, the need for *sexual* intimacy. In the past, sex kept us communicating when things got difficult. Our

relationship has never been that easy, but now we don't have that glue to keep us close. I suppose in the past six months we've made love twice.

Harriet's situation is different in that both her own and her husband's libidos have been affected by medical treatment. Surgery for a prolapsed uterus had altered her ability to have penetrative sex, while her husband's prostate surgery had made it difficult for him to have or maintain an erection. However, her husband had always associated sex with penetration, which means they now have little physical contact.

> My husband is the kind of man where one thing leads to another. If the other isn't going to happen because I'm not too keen, or it's too difficult for him, he tends to think, 'What's the point?' I find that very sad. I miss the closeness that sex gave us. It's nice to be reassured with a kiss and cuddle.
>
> When we do have sex, I am very positive about it, but it doesn't happen much these days, and, as a result of the operation I often get this acid reflux. That's *not* very sexy either.

Several women whose libido had dropped were surprised that they no longer found men sexually attractive. One example is Vivian, an interior designer in her mid-50s, who said she had been used to the sexual chemistry that came with working in a largely male environment. She was astonished at how differently she looked at men these days:

> I'm used to walking into a room, seeing a man across the room and thinking, 'I'll have a bit of that.' It doesn't happen these days because I don't have anything firing off any more. But it doesn't mean to say that I don't enjoy their company just as much. It's different, that's all.
>
> This may make me sound like I've become a dull girl, but I've had a lot of sex in my life and maybe I've had enough.

Felicity, who works in the clothing industry, echoed that experience.

> I had a lot of lovers when I was younger. In fact you could say I've had enough sex to last several lifetimes. I'm now in my mid-50s and I look at sex as being rather silly – all that humping up and down. I suppose

I feel as if I've gone beyond it, if that makes any sense. My problem is that I am in a relationship with someone I love very much. He feels bereft if I don't have sex with him. But it's coming to a point where I feel I am compromising myself if I agree.

So, fading sexual desire can be a complex matter. For some women, it's not just about a drop in libido either. Sex, as I know, can begin to hurt. A lot.

5. Horribly painful

The technical term for painful sex is vaginal atrophy.

'Two such ugly words', said 58-year-old Amanda, morosely. I agree with her. Just saying 'VA' makes my toes curl, especially as it so crudely describes what's happening to such an intimate part of a woman's body, and at such a sensitive time in her life.

VA is not something I had even heard about before I had the menopause. It's caused by a lack of oestrogen in the body, which thins and dries out the vaginal lining. The woman is unable to produce enough lubrication to make sex comfortable, and enjoyable. For many who develop VA, it can become so painful, even with the use of lubricants, that penetrative sex becomes impossible.

Yet *one in two* of us going through the menopause suffer from it from one degree to another. Yes, that's right: every second woman in the country is liable to suffer from VA during the menopause. Something to think about when you're in a room full of menopausal women.

I use the word 'suffer' loosely. If you're not having sex, you probably won't notice VA unless you have a vaginal examination (you certainly will then). But for women who are in relationships, or who really would like to stay sexually active, it can be a deeply distressing condition.

'It's true that a large percentage of women suffer from vaginal dryness, but many won't speak about it with their doctors because they're embarrassed,' Norma Goldman told me. She's a pharmacist who set up The Menopause Exchange in 1999 to provide unbiased medical and scientific information about the change of life. She added, 'Women won't even talk about it to each other. It's too sensitive.'

Rather like me, most women I spoke to with VA had no idea what was happening to them until, literally, one day sex began to hurt. One interviewee said,

I had a sense of burning after sex for some time. But I thought it was a touch of cystitis. That changed to it sometimes hurting and sometimes not. Then it just started to hurt all the time.

Fifty-seven-year-old Claire had a similar experience.

It was okay to start with. It was more like a stinging sensation than anything painful. Most of the time sex was fine. This went on for quite a few months, perhaps, even a year. Then it started to hurt a lot. It's difficult to explain, but it felt as if I was being stabbed from the inside. I had no sexual enjoyment at all. I got to the point where I couldn't bear it any more, and I had to tell my husband. He was shocked, because he had no idea.

Painful sex can lead to extremely upsetting realizations. A friend I've known since school days called me in tears to say that it had begun to hurt so much that she knew she would never be able to have sex again with her husband. She was devastated. Listening to her made me think with some melancholy of the time when we were two carefree girls full of sexual fervour, and how this had drawn to such an eye-watering conclusion for us both.

Vivian, a successful business woman in her early 60s, was also coming to terms with the fact she might never have penetrative sex again.

It's not just lying back and thinking of England. It's everywhere else I've been, and trying not to cry.

Even though sex hurt, Vivian continued to experience sexual desire, and said she would be devastated if men didn't find her attractive any more.

This means that sex had become a bit muddled these days. If I know someone loves me, it's still a real turn-on, although it does mean exploring different ways to be intimate without penetration. To be honest, I've got to the point where I can't cope with all those creams and pessaries. What a performance.

So, for me, it's more about that erotic buzz that happens when you light someone up, and they do the same to you. I want to feel that until I die.

Another interviewee said that since sex had become so painful, she was reluctant even to put her arms around her husband in case he got the wrong idea.

> We've always had such a good sexual relationship. But I daren't touch him these days in case it leads to sex. Isn't that an awful thing to say?

The issue of penetrative sex had turned Anne-Marie's relationship into a battleground. She's been with her partner for over 16 years.

> Sex has become increasingly painful for me so I really don't want it. However, my partner is crawling up the walls – sex has always been incredibly important to him – and it's becoming very difficult. I see the battle that we are now in as a destructive pattern where I feel pressurized to have sex. When I give in, I feel furious that I have betrayed myself. Then I get cross with him, and he becomes hurt.
>
> I would never call it rape. I look at that as a man forcing himself into a woman who is screaming 'No'. But I can understand the implications. It feels like rape in the moment because I don't want sex, and am doing it because I believe the relationship would break down if I don't.
>
> We both know this has got to change. I am still interested in finding out ways to have sex without penetration. But I realize no penetration ever again would be really hard for him to accept. So yes, it's tough for us both.

'Nothing,' said 66-year-old Penelope, 'can take away the guilt of no longer wanting sex.'

> We still make love once a week even though it's very uncomfortable and I don't have any libido at all. He's aware of it, but, as they say, men have their needs. I do my best, but it can't be very satisfying for him knowing that I don't enjoy it any more. I did go on HRT for six months, but when the cancer scare hit the headlines, I came off immediately and I have no intentions of going on it again.

Phoebe, also in her 60s, was very distressed by the sexual pressure she felt from her husband.

> You're only doing it for them. It's a massive problem. He's away at the moment and I feel so relieved. I can go to bed without any pressure

and just read my book. That's a dreadful thing to say. The trouble is when you don't have any libido you don't want to be touched at all. I love being cuddled but that's it.

I tell him it's nothing to do with him, it's my body. He realizes that. But it's hard for us, especially when we used to have such a good sex life. He lives in hope it will change and so do I, but I can't see how. I miss my sex drive dreadfully because I want to make it good for him.

Since coming off HRT a year or so ago, 62-year-old Jill also found sex painful. Even so, since her husband travelled a lot, she was determined to make an effort each time he came back.

We have penetrative sex about twice a week when he's home, which he normally instigates. Sometimes it becomes so painful that I've had to tell him to stop. So we use lubricants and start again slowly.

I know he'd like it more than that, but I don't. The thought of having it five times a week would be very trying – and anyway, he has to catch me in the mood. These days, this can be fleeting moments! So, I tell him, 'If you snooze you lose.' But I will make the effort because I think sex glues you together. It shouldn't, but it does.

There's no easy remedy when one partner doesn't want sex and the other does. But sex is like an invasion when you don't have any desire. One woman said, 'You might as well be a blow-up doll for the amount of pleasure you get out of it.'

But, if you like each other enough, you can get through it. We'll be looking at different ways to help better communication further on.

6. Relieved it's all over

In contrast, this final group of women spoke about the relief of no longer feeling sexual. Jackie, in her late 50s, said that when she let go of that 'dangerous' side of herself, life became more peaceful.

By dangerous, I mean not setting myself up in competition sexually. If you like, I'm no longer in that rat race of sexual attraction. Fifteen years ago, I would never have been able to talk like this. Today, even though I don't have sexual feelings, I feel happy in my skin.

Jackie added that, much to her surprise, talking about this made her realize how she had felt ashamed of no longer wanting sex. 'But I really *don't* believe there's something wrong with me,' she said. 'It's the media that make you feel like that.'

Gina, in her mid-50s, was equally relieved that sex no longer 'gnaws' at her. She admits that sex had been a risky part of her character, which had got her into 'a lot of interesting situations'.

> Yes, I'm glad it's over. Being released from that drive for sex has helped me to become connected to who I really am, rather than relating through the sexual woman I used to be. It's as if I've grown into myself. I think I'm more attractive, and I'm much more comfortable with my body.
>
> Do I miss anything about sex? Well, of course that physical buzz when you get sexually aroused. There's something immensely powerful about it. It becomes all-consuming when you reach that heightened point. It's very difficult to control or stop. Yes, I suppose I do miss that. But not how it ruled my life.

Jocelyn is in her mid-60s, and has no interest in sex either.

> It was difficult at first for my partner, but he's had health issues so he hasn't pushed it either. We often sleep together, and cuddle up, but it never turns sexual. I can't pretend I want sex even if he does. I certainly couldn't make myself.
>
> It's funny looking back on the time when I was sexual. I never imagined I would be like this. In fact I wish I could enjoy it again, but I know it's not going to happen. So there's no point in fooling myself.

For me, Meredith, a retired lawyer, summed up the relationship between sex and the older woman.

> A woman who has reached the menopause is usually just about done with family and she's facing a choice. Either she will become a granny and carry on her role of carer, or she'll find different ways to make something new out of her life. Whatever she chooses, sex will not be her main focus.

I am well aware of how painful and difficult sexual issues can be. In my own case, I know a visit to the doctor could superficially fix my lack of libido, but – I'll say it again – I don't want to be 'fixed'. I want to age naturally. I do believe this is a fundamental human right. But where does this leave my husband, especially when one considers how some men not only continue wanting and expecting sex well into their 80s and 90s, but are quite capable of siring progeny. Take, for instance, Rupert Murdoch, the founder of the News International media empire, to name one now elderly silverback remarried to a much younger woman and father again to a new family.

Fortunately, my husband and I are both very committed to our marriage and we are great friends and companions. So we are taking our time to work things out, and find different ways to be intimate with each other. Even so, similar to other interviewees, guilt for me is never far from the surface.

Gay relationships

I was curious to know if lesbian partnerships have similar experiences of conflict when it comes to the loss of sex. Sixty-two-year-old Lara has been with her partner for three years and told me she thought it was easier for lesbians.

> Both of us have been through the menopause, and neither of us feels particularly sexual any more. So there's not the same sexual expectation that a husband will have. For us, a secure relationship is not dependent on sex, and it's not what our relationship has been built on. I tend to look at my loss of sexual drive as 'Shit happens. No big deal.' So does my partner.
>
> We have lots of other ways of demonstrating intimacy and love to each other and we really enjoy each other's company.

I asked 60-year-old Mandy if she misses sex.

> It's funny you should ask. We are good friends with a lesbian couple who have recently met, and they are having a fantastic time sexually. I do catch myself thinking it must be quite nice to have that added dimension in your relationship. I don't lose sleep over it, but I do feel that I have lost something. Some aspect of my physicality has failed, in the sense that it has ceased to function. I am aware that some women continue to have a sexual drive after the menopause, and wonder why I'm not one of them. But this is a personal thing, and it doesn't affect my relationship.

Claudia is also in her early 60s and has been in a civil partnership with her partner Judi for a couple of years. She hasn't felt sexual desire since she went through the menopause in her mid-50s, and has no sense of guilt.

> When I met Judi there was an immediate soul connection between us. It's wasn't a sexual thing for me, although this did change. I suppose you could say I grew to be sexual with her. It started off with us kissing, and other things developed from there. I was quite surprised that I felt anything actually. It didn't last that long though. Quite quickly our relationship shifted away from being sexual into one of deep intimacy and friendship. I like being with someone who doesn't judge me for what I am sexually, who has that sexual need for me. I don't want all that sexual drama any more. I had enough it of it in my past.
>
> Instead, I like the reality of what we have together. We inspire and support each other in whatever we are doing. I like myself too. I don't have to be entertained. It's not about being boring, it's about being peaceful. People get that confused.

It's good to hear how these gay women are with supportive partners who, of course, being older females themselves, are experiencing similar sexual changes. But as we've already found in this exploration of the realities of the menopause, talking about sexual changes can be much more difficult for heterosexual couples.

The need for good communication

I asked interviewees what helped them deal with sexual differences that developed in their relationship. 'It's about taking a deep breath and being honest,' said 57-year-old Philippa.

> I'm fortunate that my husband is open and supportive. We enjoy each other's company and want to make our relationship work. Communicating has helped us to find out what's okay for us both, but it's not easy.
>
> It was getting very dodgy between us a year-and-a-half ago. He couldn't understand what I was going through, and took my loss of libido as a personal rejection. It was also interesting how your time frame goes out when you start feeling pressurized. He kept on saying it had been months since we'd had sex. I kept saying, 'No, it hasn't. It's only been a few days.' The truth lay somewhere in between.

Eventually I told him we couldn't go on like this – we had to do something about it. That changed everything. We sat down and talked on and off for a whole day. We said some pretty difficult things to each other, which meant that at times we needed to walk away and have a cup of tea separately, and then we'd come back and start again. I would listen to him, and then he would listen to me. It's tough, but if you want to move forward in your relationship and for it to survive, you *have* to do this.

Fifty-eight-year-old Pamela said that it made a difference to understand deeper issues that were going on with both her and her partner.

Both of us are aware of other underlying psychological issues that may not be helping. As a child, he felt deprived of his mother's love, and never had enough access to her physically. I had an intrusive mother who never respected my boundaries. So, for him it's about adult sex stuff intertwined with the little boy needing breast. For me, it's someone coming inside me who has not been invited.

It's been just as complex for 57-year-old Shirley. The mother of four children, she had never felt comfortable with her sexuality, but this became more of an issue when the menopause arrived. Talking to a therapist helped her to understand that her sexual ambivalence was connected to an overbearing father who, wanting a son, never recognized her femininity.

I realized that I've lived my life feeling like an asexual being – which is strange to say when I've been married for 30 years and have four children. Understanding how my father's attitude affected me hasn't made me reach for the HRT, but it's helped me to be much more receptive to my husband. Even though I still don't want sex, it has made a huge difference to the way we listen to each other.

Fifty-eight-year-old Susie and her partner decided to go to a tantric sex workshop to help them overcome their difficulties.

Our sex life was quite difficult when we first got together. He'd been in a sexless marriage for years, and it had made him quite nervous. We found going to tantric sex workshops in Switzerland very helpful. It takes the stress off because you're taught various techniques that help you to understand the importance of making love rather than just going through the motions. Without that, I think we'd be in real trouble now. It helped him to understand that sex isn't just about penetration. He has always been caught up on that.

I think the best way to judge sex is how you feel afterwards. Sometimes I agree because I know he's desperate for it. But I am aware if I let this happen too often I would start to feel resentful. At other times I can feel very connected, and it's got nothing to do with orgasm. It's just nice. Sometimes we'll start and it doesn't go anywhere and we stop, and that's okay too.

However, for some couples, discussing personal issues let alone sexual ones is out of the question. Jan sounded in despair when she told me how impossible it was to talk to her husband about what was happening to her.

I never know what he wants. He's very closed about sex. I've tried talking to him, but it never gets very far. I would love this to change. I would love to understand where he's at, because this would help me to know how to be more intimate with him. We need to find ways to deal with what's happening to us.

Professor Julie Winterich, who we've met before, emphasized how important good communication is as a woman goes through the menopause. She told me that even though women might be experiencing symptoms such as vaginal dryness, they are much more affected by what is happening within their relationship. Women in good relationships, who are able to talk openly to their partners, find ways to adapt to sexual changes they are experiencing. She added, 'No surprise, women in poor relationships blame their symptoms or other social and health issues for the sexual difficulties they were having, and feel the added stress of having to "deal" with their partners who complained about it.'

Liz Copestake is a sex therapist and member of the British Association for Sexual and Relationship Therapy (BASPT). She is amazed at how little couples – especially those married for 30 years and more – know about the sexual and psychological changes that happen during the menopause. Her work more often than not is helping these older couples to understand new ways to be intimate with each other.

There's lots of ways to be close, without necessarily having penetration, but there does need to be a willingness to explore different things that work for the couple.

For example, the skin is one of the biggest sex organs we have, and lying together naked can produce the same oxytocins as making love. This basic education can help couples to find a way to continue to express their love for each other without getting caught up on how sex is portrayed in the media.

Liz also encourages couples to talk honestly to each other and to listen to what's really being said, so that they can learn to face their fears and doubts together.

The fact that a couple comes to therapy means they both want to make some kind of effort, and I do whatever I can to support this. For example, male clients may say they want sex 500 times a day, but when you get down to it what they really want is emotional connection. They misinterpret their wife's lack of interest as rejection. She's not necessarily rejecting him; she's just not interested in sex, which is different – for her anyway. Once men understand this, it changes things.

Of course sexual intercourse is important to some people. But I do think women can get hung up on thinking that if they don't continue to have sex their husband will walk out. I had one client who was convinced this was all her husband wanted. He, on the other hand, kept telling her what *he* wanted was hugs and cuddles. That was enough for him, but she couldn't hear it. It took months of therapy for her to finally realize it was okay and he wasn't going to leave her.

As Liz Copestake points out, sex and menopause is a complex issue. It needs time and patience, especially when couples have never spoken about sex, or indeed intimacy, before.

Sexual differences

Listening to the stories that make up this book brought home to me how very different men and women are sexually. As we've heard, women on the whole seem much less bothered than men as their interest in sex changes. Where, then, does that leave the men? And if you want to stay together, and sexually faithful, what do you do?

That brings us to another taboo 'M' word, masturbation.

Male masturbation and sex toys

Although studies say that 95 per cent of men masturbate, and continue to do so throughout their sexual lives, few women I spoke to seemed explicitly aware of their partners' masturbating – although there did seem to be a general acceptance that they probably did.

However, two women did tell me they had encouraged their partners to masturbate to take the pressure off them sexually. Not that it always worked. 'I've told him to masturbate, but he doesn't want to. He wants to have sex with me,' said one.

The other had the same experience.

> I know he masturbates to compensate, because he has told me he does. But he doesn't find it much good. The point is, he wants to have an intimate relationship with me, which is very tough on us both. He also realized that although he could go and find someone else, sooner or later she'll have a menopause too. So, there's not much point in that either.

Masturbation can raise deeper personal issues, especially when there's a lack of connection between partners. One man in his mid-50s told me his wife had gone through the menopause and no longer wanted sex, but wouldn't talk about it. To compensate, he masturbated regularly, but he also regarded what he was doing as being unfaithful. So, although he experienced sexual release, it left him feeling distressed, confused and guilty. He did, however, wonder whether this sexual guilt might be a leftover from being sent to Catholic boarding school aged nine. I felt very sad for him, and it made me wonder how many other men of similar age were feeling shamed by a perfectly normal and natural need for sexual release.

I might add at this point, especially for any male readers, that masturbation is not only a natural thing to do, but it might be good for you as you get older. A 2009 study in the *British Journal of Urology International* suggests that regular sexual activity, meaning here a combination of sexual intercourse and masturbation more than ten times a month, may have a small protective effect against prostate cancer for men over 50. The report speculated that ejaculation might help remove toxins, but did note that further research was needed.

I also spoke to a woman whose husband regularly uses a 'vagina' sex toy. She, herself, is postmenopausal and no longer interested in sex. As a couple, they've always been very close and have never had secrets from each other, but she was shocked when he first told her about it.

> However, when I thought about it, I felt rather touched that he'd rather use something like this than have an affair, or see a prostitute. Sex has always meant a lot to him, much more than it has to me, so how can I be moralistic about it? Actually, I really respect the fact that he told me. It's such a taboo thing. But it does make me sad to think that my lack of interest in sex these days has pushed him into this. He told me that if we started having sex again, the sex toy would go. I believe him. I think.

I appreciate that many women might find the thought of their husbands and partners masturbating or using a sex toy uncomfortable or even disgusting. But it's a fact of life that most men masturbate, even when they are having a satisfying sex life. It's up to you whether you want to talk to your partner about it.

Female masturbation and sex toys

But, masturbation is not just about men's sexual release. Women masturbate too, although much less than their male counterparts. An American study conducted in 2004 says that one in five women between the ages of 18 and 60 masturbate at least once a week.

Nearly 60 per cent of those women who do masturbate were using a sex toy at the time of the research. Women aged between 55 and 60 were just as likely to have used a sex toy at some point in their life, but far fewer were using them when they took part in the study. Surprisingly (to me anyway), the report also found that the highest percentage of women (of all ages) who used sex toys were in a relationship, although they weren't using them as a substitute for sex with their partners.

Fifty-five-year-old Carolyn was very open about the way she masturbates, and she uses sex toys as well as enjoying a good sex life with her partner. They've been together for five years. She told me, 'I look at myself as having a dual relationship: sex with my partner, and sex with myself.' She continued,

> I consider masturbation a celebration of me. So there's this whole side of me which is much freer and more satisfied than it's ever been. He [my partner] knows about it, although we don't often talk about

it. In fact, it's him that buys me different lubricants and sex toys. I
have three at the moment. But we don't use them together. They are
my toys.

It depends how often I use them. Sometimes it's once a week,
sometimes once a fortnight, and we make love together every couple
of weeks. Mind you, how often we make love has diminished since
we started doing up our new house. It's amazing how things like
painting and gardening detract from your sex life.

Several more women told me that masturbation and sex toys had
always been an important part of their sex life. However, most
noticed a loss of interest as soon as they reached the menopause.
One said, 'I keep seeing my toys in my underwear drawer, but these
days I can't be bothered with them.' Another woman in her late 50s
said she was surprised that masturbating no longer appealed. 'I don't
seem interested any more. That's a big change for me, especially as
I've been in a non-sexual relationship with my husband for a long
time.'

Other women continue to masturbate regularly, such as Rosemary,
who is in her 60s. Her husband is in a care home, and she's been
on her own for several years. She looks at masturbation as a gift to
herself.

If I find it hard to sleep I will masturbate, so I know I haven't dried
up. It's pleasurable for me, and actually it's a relief that I don't
have to provide pleasure for a man. If I found a lover, sex would be
a bonus. But that's not the reason I would have a man in my life,
certainly not these days.

It's one thing to have a positive relation with masturbation. But
pornography is more complicated.

Pornography

Pornography used to be limited to the odd 'dirty book' and those
glossy magazines with big-breasted girls on the front cover, found
on the top shelf at the local tobacconist. Today, of course it's far
more easily accessible – in fact, spectacularly so. There are over
500 million pages of pornography on the internet, and according to
UK statistics, internet porn is accessed by an estimated 33 per cent
of all internet users. (Indeed, much of the technical development of

the entire internet has been driven by the popularity of pornography.) A third of men say they would never openly confess to watching it, and nearly nine in ten delete their browsing history as soon as they've watched it. The vast majority of men watch pornography only when they are alone.

I've not been able to find statistics on how many men married to menopausal women use internet porn. But I would imagine quite a number. Only one woman talked about what it was like to discover that her husband was regularly using it. She was horrified.

> When I discovered what he was up to, I felt a surge of disgust towards him. I couldn't believe he would do something like that. I thought we had a great relationship. Okay, sex wasn't that good any more, but we have three grown-up children, and a grandchild on the way. I couldn't get my head around why he would want to do something like this. It's created a lot of mistrust and conflict between us.

Wendy Maltz, the American sex therapist, is also the author of *The Porn Trap*. She says it can become very difficult when older women find their husbands are using porn to compensate for a lack of sex.

> Some men might use porn for a short while and then not bother again, others can become addicted. The danger is the way men can condition themselves to become less emotionally available when they use pornography, and less attracted to their partner.

I asked Wendy what was the best way for a couple to deal with this. 'To start with, a woman can ask her partner to stop using porn. But as reasonable as it may be to her, this approach doesn't always work', she told me.

> You have to understand how tremendously attractive today's pornography is to many men. It's available anytime, anywhere, in all varieties. It's used to enhance masturbation and intensify orgasm. Porn delivers a *faux* way of having sex with women. Some men use it to increase their sense of masculine power through fantasy. In addition, porn is often used to create a drug-like experience. It spikes the release of pleasure chemicals in the brain, such as dopamine and testosterone. Using porn can be as engaging as gambling or taking drugs.

Wendy pointed out that when a man becomes strongly attached or addicted to pornography, his partner will often sense there is something wrong, and become suspicious. If his porn use is discovered, she may understandably feel betrayed, even traumatized. But if she becomes angry and accusatory, her intense reaction can lead to a destructive pattern of behaviour for the couple.

> The woman's upset can result in her husband or partner becoming more secretive and emotionally distant. And the more isolated and ashamed he feels, the more he may continue to betray her sexually by continuing his porn use.

Wendy said that stopping the use of porn is not easy. Many men need outside support and counselling help to succeed.

> It's common for men to promise to stop using porn once they have been discovered. But even when they have good intentions, many men often are unable to succeed on their own. The couple needs to learn how to work together to understand each other's feelings about porn, address the porn problem, and ultimately improve their communication and sexual intimacy.

Certainly not all men use pornography or become addicted. However, when pornography becomes a problem, couples, as Wendy mentioned, can find counselling helpful. I have listed some helpful contacts and resources at the end of the book.

Affairs

The menopause is not just about a mechanical breakdown in the sex department. It also coincides with the much deeper and broader crises that both sexes can go through in midlife. Relationships can go stale, particularly when children leave home. It can be a particularly dodgy time emotionally for a man who finds it hard to accept his own ageing process, and who might have a wife no longer bothered about sex any more. All too often he turns to another woman to revive the passion and excitement that's disappeared from his life.

The discovery of an affair seldom passes quietly. Often when a woman finds out about her partner's infidelities, she will feel dreadfully betrayed – sometimes putting the relationship beyond salvation. But when I have talked to men about infidelity, I have come to realize most really *don't* set out to be disloyal. Rather they were more often feeling isolated, lonely, confused or generally unhappy in their relationship, and in need of warm, loving connection.

I must add that I am not condoning infidelity. But, speaking with my psychotherapist's hat on, when it does happen I believe it is always an expression of other underlying problems that haven't been addressed. When things blow open, a couple is forced to choose consciously whether they want to grow old together.

Facing a further 30 years with someone you realize you don't want to be with any more can feel like a life sentence, and according to national statistics, many couples, as we will discover further on in this chapter, are deciding to go their separate ways.

Several women talked to me about the emotional trauma of discovering their husband's infidelity. Fifty-five-year-old Vanessa's story is typical.

> I'm on HRT for medical reasons, but it does mean we've never hit sexual problems as such – although I will admit sex had got rather perfunctory and dull. I think he had this affair because he has found the ageing process far more difficult than me.
>
> He turned 50 at the same time as our sons were leaving home and heading out into the world. I think he felt jealous that they had lots of sex and opportunities, and he didn't. For my part, I was delighted they had finally left home. I felt I had done a good job and it was time for something new in my life. I was horrified when my husband said at one point that he wished we'd had more children so he could carry on watching them play sports and being part of the school community. The thought appals me.

Vanessa's biggest issue was realizing that the 'other' woman was only a few years younger than herself.

> It would have been easier to cope with if she'd been much younger, or he'd had a one-off fling with some secretary. But to have to face the fact that the affair lasted over two years, and he stayed friends with her after it was over, has been very difficult. To me, emotional infidelity is far worse than physical infidelity.

However, in Vanessa's case, something positive has come from this turmoil. It has forced her and husband to talk to each other, and to reassess what they both really want.

Realizing someone else wanted him – wanted to have sex with him – made me look at him in a new light, and to think about whether I really wanted him myself.

He, on the other hand, is mortified about what he's done, and is desperate for our marriage to continue. He's even gone to counselling to see if he can sort himself out and has promised never to see or make contact with that woman again.

So, it's certainly made us re-examine our relationship, even where we want to live, and what we want to do with our lives. This may or may not mean we stay together. Although we are now at a stage of attempted normality, for me it's far too early to make that kind of decision.

Barely one in three marriages survive extramarital affairs, and any couples who've gone through this will know that the real test of the relationship only begins after the affair is over.

Divorce

Although Britain's overall divorce rate has fallen by 16 per cent since 1998, at the same time the number of what some people now call 'Saga divorces' – couples separating after 30 and 40 years of marriage – has risen by 19 per cent (Saga being a British company that has done very well out of marketing holidays and insurance to the over-50s). Relate, the national organization which provides support for relationships in difficulty, says women now instigate seven out of ten of these Saga divorces. While men tend to leave their wives for another woman, women leave because they want independence.

However, according to the UK's Health Promotion Agency, there's another reason for the increase in Saga divorces. This concerns the soaring rates of sexually transmitted diseases (STDs) in the over-50s who seem to be having sex with new partners. This includes such delights as syphilis, herpes, Chlamydia, genital warts, gonorrhoea and also HIV. It's disturbing to learn that the HIV infection rate in older people has more than doubled in the past seven years.

Inadequate sexual health information for the baby-boomer generation means that many are unaware of the dangers of catching these STDs, as *Saga Magazine* discovered when it ran a survey about sex in later life. It found that ten per cent of sexually active people over 50 say they are not practising safe sex, but they have no idea that they are putting themselves at risk – or their spouse if they have one.

So be warned. And use a condom.

Prostitution

Looking at sexual differences between men and women made me think, again (recalling my interview with Sandra in Chapter 2) about prostitution.

A UK Government report published in 2010 suggests that one in ten men have visited a prostitute at some point in their lives. An international survey in the US looked into the reasons why men used prostitution. One in three said they needed to satisfy an immediate sexual urge, or just did it for pleasure. Twenty per cent were not having their needs met in their current relationship. Fifteen per cent did it for convenience, eight per cent for the thrill, and an interestingly low figure of just three per cent were addicted or acted out of compulsion. Sixty per cent found sex through brothels, 27 per cent used the internet, just over a half met prostitutes in private flats, just under half went to massage parlours, a third used escort agencies, and just over one in four went to saunas.

None of the women I interviewed acknowledged knowing that their partners or husbands had gone to prostitutes. So to find out from the horse's mouth, as it were, I asked Sandra, who we heard from in the last chapter, what she thought older men were looking for. She had no idea how common it was for men married to menopausal women to be paying for sex, but said she suspected it was a significant number.

It must be hard for a man when his wife doesn't want sex any more, and he isn't into porn. I would guess most wives don't know, but I can understand why men wouldn't say anything. Why would you make your relationship even more stressful?

A lot of older men I've known make long-term arrangements. They want to feel comfortable and to talk. You need to know someone to be able to do that. Yes, sometimes they do fall in love with you, but it's very rare for a sex worker to go there with them on that. It gets too difficult and complicated.

It's important to understand that for any sex worker, it's about getting the job done as quickly as possible. It's not about emotional connection or involvement. That's not our job. My 'no-frills' fee used to be 50 pounds for an hour, but I also saw what I did as providing a form of therapy. You had to be a good listener as well.

I can quite understand how horrified many women would be if they found their husbands and partner were visiting a prostitute. I know I would certainly struggle with it. But I found Sandra so refreshingly down to earth and honest that I could understand why men would have gone to her. However, it was important for me to know that Sandra was in full control of her life.

It's a different story for many sex workers, who have either been coerced into prostitution by abusive partners or pimps, or who are victims of sex trafficking. A 2010 report from Britain's Association of Chief Police Officers estimated that around 30,000 women work in what's technically termed off-street prostitution in England and Wales, of whom 17,000 were from outside the UK, and over 2,500 trafficked from countries such as China, South East Asia and Eastern Europe.

Menopause power!

We are now going to change gear completely to talk about a new breed of women who, perhaps with the help of HRT (and hopefully practising safe sex), are enjoying a completely different menopause to that of their mothers. Many are from the 600,000 older women in the UK who are divorced, widowed or have never been married.

In my early 40s, recalling that wonderful 1989 film about a British teacher who finds romance on a Greek island, I had my own Shirley Valentine moment in Greece with Andreas. And no, he wasn't a waiter, nor was he years younger than me, although he certainly did possess an air of Mediterranean male superiority. Remembering him through the eyes of the postmenopausal woman I am today makes me feel rather wistful.

But being a Shirley Valentine is old hat. These days it's about being *cougars* – the name given to older women who actively seek out sex with significantly younger men – or *SWOFTIES*: Single Women Over Fifty, who like clubbing, tweeting and exotic holidays, etc. According to a study commissioned in 2010 for the Department of Work and Pensions, SWOFTIES have never been happier.

None of the women I spoke to admitted to being a cougar, but several fell into the SWOFTY category. They were financially independent, either through their own efforts or through hefty divorce settlements. They took care of their health, and had no intention of living in enforced celibacy just because they didn't have a regular partner.

However, meeting men of a similar age is notoriously difficult for older women. As one friend in her mid-50s commented to me wryly, 'Men of my age are like parking meters: either broken or taken.' It does seem to be true. I have many wonderful, vibrant, single and divorced girlfriends, but where are the men? Remarried, I suspect, to younger women, and having another round of children.

To compensate, some older women turn to younger lovers, or remarry much older men. Age-gap relationships can be very successful. However, a 2010 German study from the Max Planck Institute for Demographic Research does threaten to spoil the fun. It suggests that not only do older husbands shorten a woman's life span (perhaps they bore their wives to death) but younger husbands are even more lethal to her health. The reason for this, says the study, is that marriage to a much younger man falls outside the social norm, which could in turn create more emotional stress for the woman.

My interpretation of this is that that the older wife spends her life looking over her shoulder in case her paramour is eyeing up someone nearer his own age, and knowing that it really is only a question of time before he's off. Let's face it: it's as hard for homo sapiens males bursting with testosterone to ignore the call of evolution as it is for male gorillas.

The German study concludes that the best partner for a woman is someone of her own age. But, it also provides an astonishing contrast to the impact on the woman, in that a man's life expectancy increases when he's married to a much younger woman. So, it seems that marriage is life-enhancing for men, and can be life-shortening for women. How unfair.

SWOFTIES abroad

The lack of same-aged male partners means that some menopausal SWOFTIES are travelling abroad to find lovers. One woman I know met her husband when he served her a drink in a small bar in the Middle East. Another met her Indian husband on a beach in Goa. Some of these relationships are very successful; others are disastrous. One woman I know invested all her savings into her Egyptian lover's business. She never saw him or her money again.

The fact that many SWOFTIES are a soft touch (or, let's be honest, having a good time sexually with local young men) is making travelling alone more difficult. A friend in her early 50s who spends a lot of time in West Africa finds it impossible to walk on any beach unless it's part of a hotel complex. She told me, 'You are constantly being harassed by young men expecting a meal and a shag.'

It's not just happening abroad. Some women I spoke to said they are being targeted through internet dating sites. One woman in her 60s told me how she had been pestered by emails from an 18-year-old boy. 'I couldn't shake him off,' she said. 'I kept asking him why he should be interested in someone of my age. He replied that he wanted to have sex with me. I know he was after something else too, like money.'

Apparently there's also a new game in town. A friend overheard several young men laughing about older women as if they were sport to them. She told me, 'They were planning a good *grab-a-granny* night out, and if they got the woman to pay, so much the better.'

As long as you are in control of what's happening, it's great to enjoy yourself as an independent mature woman. But do take care. Put a condom in your handbag, and keep your wits about you. I've listened to many a doleful tale about an older woman believing she had found Mr Right in some far-flung exotic country, only to have her heart broken and her bank account emptied.

To summarize this chapter, I hope you now have a much better overall understanding of what happens with the mechanics of sex during the menopause. The range of sexual change, whether this means an increase in libido or the complete loss of desire, is a *normal* expression of what's happening to the hormone production in the ovaries. If sex becomes a problem, some women choose to go down the HRT route. Others are not prepared to take artificial hormones even if this means that their libido dies completely.

Sexual changes, by the very fact that they mark the time when a woman begins to age, do create issues in relationships, and often bring out sexual differences between men and women. As I've said before, if you are having problems and you can't talk to each other about it, do seek help from a counselling professional.

Finally, the divorce rate in the baby-boomer generation is rapidly increasing. Many are having sex with new partners, unaware of the risks of sexually transmitted diseases. So, have a good time. But, again, do be careful. Watch out for your heart and your bank balance.

Now we've looked at different aspects of sexual changes, it's time to move on to the next dimension of the M-word: meaning.

CHAPTER 4

Meaning and the menopause

This M-word chapter focuses on how meaning and purpose change as we move through the menopause. Some women describe this time as a practical opportunity for personal growth and development. Others see it somehow as a reflective, and perhaps more mystical or spiritual experience. I accept that the concept of spirituality isn't necessarily for everyone. Even so, almost without exception, the women I interviewed spoke of an awareness of being somehow called to a deeper part of themselves. That has certainly been true for me.

Alexandra Pope, co-author of *The Pill: Are You Sure it's For You*, told me how important it was for an older woman to find meaning and purpose in her life.

> I think a lot of women become depressed at this time of their lives. They believe life doesn't have anything for them any more, so they end up just getting through each day. They may have a partner who doesn't value them, their outer beauty has gone, and they believe they haven't got anything to measure themselves against any more. That's sad. This can be an incredibly rich time for a woman. But you need to find something to make you feel valued for who you are, and what you can contribute.

Wendy Maltz, the American sex therapist, agrees.

> As we grow older we need to move away from associating our sexuality with our body image. You can't let common changes like saggy breasts, larger bellies, and a few hanging folds of skin ruin your life. You'll only get more disappointed with time. We need to focus more on our inner essence – connections of the heart, and pleasurable skin and organ sensations.

To nurture this inner essence, some women I interviewed for this book go regularly to spiritual growth and personal development workshops. Some have chosen to do prayer or meditation retreats. Some have taken up chanting, singing or playing music and dancing. Others have gone into therapy to deal, for example, with childhood issues which they have at last realized lie at the root of things that still bother them. Some have gone to astrologers to have their birth chart done. Some have found help through spiritual and religious books. Others have found support through women's groups and organizations. Others again have gone to university or night school to retrain in a different occupation, or just for the sheer enjoyment of learning.

The inner call

The way we become conscious of the need to do things differently is a very individual experience. For some women it is a slowly growing awareness. For others, as in my case, it can be more like an alarm clock clanging loudly in the ear.

My own alarm went off some time before the menopause. Although I had had my fair share of lovers, I was metaphorically asleep until my mid-30s. I had no idea who I was or what I was capable of. As a result, I made some very poor life choices, and caused a lot of anguish to people who didn't deserve it. These were hard and painful lessons in understanding and respecting the power of taking action and then living with the consequences.

I was rudely shaken awake after crash-landing in a light aircraft at the age of 36, and believing I was going to die. It forced me to look at myself, and to reassess everything that mattered. Since then, my spiritual growth has been the most important thing in my life. But I've noticed there's a different quality to this now that I have become a postmenopausal woman. It's hard to put into words, but it feels as if a deepening *has* taken place, a *sinking into* who I really am.

That doesn't mean to say I won't continue to wilt over the changes that face me daily in the mirror as well as in the bedroom. It's part of normal life for me these days, but it doesn't stand in the way of my getting on with who I want to become.

I love the notion that I have arrived at the time of my life where I can nurture who I am inside. Nevertheless, the build-up to this acceptance has been at times both frightening and distressing. Most of us don't immediately take on board that the physical changes we go through during the menopause coincide, and often collide, with the existential crisis that midlife – yet another M-word – brings anyway.

I use 'existential' in this context as the sense of becoming increasingly conscious of a need to do things differently. This may be triggered by growing feelings of grief, boredom, loss, anxiety, fear of the future, or just an underlying unease that things 'aren't somehow quite right'. Having reached – and gone through – my own midlife crisis, I can see how it has forced me to change from being the self-obsessed, hedonistic young woman I was to someone who wants to contribute something worthwhile to others, and to care for the natural world. This midlife transition is such an important part of our psychological and spiritual development as women that I think it's important to explore what happens in a little more detail.

Midlife: a psychological crisis

The psychology of life transitions, as I found out as a psychotherapist, is a vast, complex area. There are as many models out there to help us understand this, I sometimes feel, as there are psychotherapists in the known universe – and that's a lot. However, for me, Erik Erikson's 'lifespan' development framework is one of the simplest and most effective models of understanding.

Erikson was an American psychologist who saw the human lifespan as an ever-evolving state, constantly challenging us to grow and mature. Midlife, he suggested, was especially important as a time to consider our contribution to family, community, work and society. As the following chart shows, how we embrace these responsibilities depends on our psychological programming during childhood. For example, according to Erikson, a person who has positive childhood experiences is able to develop trust. Trust helps us to form strong bonds with others as we go through life, and to develop self-esteem. A child who has negative experiences finds it difficult or impossible to develop trust. This makes it much more difficult to forge healthy relationships or accept personal responsibility. Nevertheless, each life stage, from infancy to old age, continues to provide opportunity for change.

Midlife itself, said Erikson, challenges us to develop creativity or to stagnate, with creativity defined as the selfless ways that people choose to contribute to the world as they mature, rather than languishing in the triviality of their own lives. He believed that when a person truly embraces their creativity, they develop a far deeper sense of personal integrity.

Erickson's chart of the human psychological lifespan

Infancy 0–1 years	Trust vs. distrust
Infancy 2 years	Autonomy vs. shame and doubt
Early childhood 3–5 years	Initiative vs. guilt
Middle childhood 6–11 years	Industry vs. inferiority
Adolescence 12–20 years	Identity vs. role confusion
Young adulthood 20s and 30s	Intimacy vs. isolation
Middle adulthood 40s and 50s	Productive creativity vs. stagnation
Late adulthood 60s and over	Integrity vs. despair

Midlife: a spiritual process

But, midlife is not just a psychological process. 'Every midlife crisis', wrote Carl Jung, the great twentieth-century Swiss psychiatrist, 'is a spiritual crisis, where we are called to die to the old self (ego) . . . and liberate the new man or woman within us.'

Jung divided life into two main phases, simply titled morning and afternoon. Morning, said Jung, is when we relate to our external world and develop our egos accordingly. Afternoon is when we turn towards our inner world and have the opportunity to develop our true selves. Jung was aware that this transition is challenging, and likened it to a difficult birth. In *Stages of Life*, he writes, 'We take this step with the false presuppositions that our truths and ideas will serve as hitherto. But we cannot live the afternoon of life according to the programme of life's morning.'

The psychoanalyst Jolande Jacobi, a student of Jung, also spoke of midlife as a difficult birth. 'Like a seed growing into a tree,' she wrote, 'life unfolds stage by stage. Triumphant ascent, collapse, crises, failures, and new beginnings strew the way.'

This reminds me of the extraordinary life of Helen Keller, who more than a hundred years ago in the US was the first deaf and blind person ever to gain a degree. She went on to become an internationally famous speaker and author, and said,

Character cannot be developed in ease and quiet. Only through experience of trial and suffering can the soul be strengthened, vision cleared, ambition inspired, and success achieved.

Menopause: the struggle

Without wishing to belittle men's very real experiences of midlife, for a woman this is a stage full with ends and beginnings. Not only must we confront the death of our fertility and how we have been defined sexually; to be ourselves, we have to break away from cultural perceptions of how an older woman should be.

The American psychotherapist and theologian Thomas Moore writes in *Dark Nights of the Soul*:

> For many women the shift from being the bountiful mother to being a person in search of her essence is a difficult period of change. Naturally, people admire the selflessness of the caring mother, but what's to admire in the search for the self? This effort will look narcissistic and far from virtuous.
>
> When you make the important move to find your essence, you will probably have to do it alone. You may have to accept that you will be misread and under-appreciated. Certainly your family have to adjust.

Bonnie Horrigan, author of *Red Moon Passage*, notes that too many women today struggle alone with these momentous changes, unable to make sense of them because they no longer have older, prudent mentors to whom they can turn.

Horrigan, director of the Society of Shamanic Practitioners, an international group dedicated to re-emergence of spiritual healing in Western culture, helps women to see the menopause as a journey for the soul, led in her interpretation of what happens by the archetypes of the seeker, destroyer, lover and creator. (Carl Jung explained archetypes as primordial characters within us, or 'universal images that have existed since the remotest times'.) In Horrigan's understanding, the role of the seeker within us is to call us to our spirit. The destroyer leads us through the grieving process of saying goodbye to the woman we were. The lover helps us to recognize what we truly cherish. Finally, the creator is about transforming ourselves into a new – and wiser – way of being. She writes:

When we have the courage to actually be who we are, then we transform our personal kingdom. The ripple effect helps to transform the larger kingdom.

In order to make a difference in the world, you need to do your own work. You need to take your own journey and face your own dragons and find your own treasures.

Horrigan believes that when we find our inner treasure, we know who we are and are able to recognize our personal truth. This helps us to find our calling and to develop our own distinctive gifts that we can use in the world. But, she added,

If people fail to do that, if they get into performance or what the management literature says, they end up being a good copy of someone else, and there is an empty space where their own unique gifts could be.

Alexandra Pope told me how difficult it can be to break away from stereotypical images of the maiden or the mother. 'But,' she added, 'menopausal women need to go beyond this.'

The changes that happen during the menopause take a woman much deeper into herself, and challenge her to accept herself in a new way. That's the nature of a spiritual journey. Spiritual practice is about delivering yourself deep into a place of being who you are.

Alexandra also believes – and her thinking overlaps here with my own research into end-of-life experiences for both men and women – that if a woman hasn't made peace with herself by the time she reaches the menopause (as we've discovered, also a form of death after all), there is going to be trouble.

You'll be taken over by the menopause as a way of escaping from what you are really feeling. When you enter this new stage of life, there's an opportunity to experience spiritual transition – to be your authentic self. But you need emotional intelligence to do it. If you haven't worked on yourself, you can't process the losses you will feel, and you won't have the inner resources to draw on.

Angie, the yoga teacher we met in Chapter 1, also believed it was vital to be prepared for what is coming.

> Society indulges people who don't want to grow old. But if you
> buy into this, or you spend all your time looking into a future that
> can't exist, you waste what precious life you have. What matters
> is to draw on your losses, bereavements, disappointments and
> those unexpected smacks around the face, and make the best of
> life that you can. When you hit the menopause, it tells you you're
> entering your last phase of life. So you may as well make the most
> of it.

In short, we *have* to jettison the perception that, once the menopause
arrives, we're only good for the scrap heap.

Menopause: a sacred state

Professor Paula Gunn Allen, an American Indian scholar and poet,
describes this transition in *Red Moon Passage* as a 'sacred state', a
profoundly spiritual as well as physical experience, similar to when
a woman is entering puberty or pregnancy:

> Women are 'different' during these times. Being in a sacred state
> means that you are open or porous, and because of that, energies
> from the non-physical world can permeate your consciousness. [But]
> consciousness is not just in your mind as so many people think: it
> involves the entire body.

For me, becoming conscious of what was happening during the
menopause meant that I spent several years in a kind of twilight
zone, feeling as if I was standing at a threshold where I still had one
foot in the past, and was very tentatively extending my big toe into
the waters of older age. Sometimes I would snatch my toe back,
feeling far too young for this to be happening. At other times I felt
the urge to go for a paddle. But all the time I could feel energies in
my body shifting, becoming aware that something far bigger than
'old me' was at stake. This 'old me' had to make way for a wiser self
to become my new inner companion. It forced me to become more
discerning about who I was, and to accept that although I couldn't
change things in the past that I wish I hadn't done, I could at least
learn from them, and find ways to atone for them.

In her book, *Crones Don't Whine*, Jean Shinoda Bolen uses the
terminology of 'crone' to describe the menopausal woman who's
gone on her own inner quest, to confront self-deception, fear and

doubt, and who is now ready to put wisdom and discernment to good use.

> Crones are women who learn from experience and can apply past lessons to present choices. Seeing the consequences of their actions teaches them lessons they take to heart. They are women who are passionate, courageous and principled, yet [who] were once heedless of the harm they could cause by acting on impulse.

So far, maturing has been an extraordinary adventure for me. But, similar to many others on the same journey, it hasn't been an easy task. Lesley Kenton writes in *Passage to Power* that she had to learn 'brand new languages' in order to live in the completely new world that emerged from the chaos of her own menopause.

> What did I gain from all this? Only the absolute knowing that there is an incredible natural order which regulates our lives even when we perceive ourselves to be in total disarray. Within this order is to be found a quality of love and a compassion that goes far beyond anything I could ever have imagined. It continually asks that we venture deep into the realm of wisdom and it knows exactly what is right and necessary from one moment to the next in our lives.

Love and self-healing

There may be readers of a rational, scientific mind who would wish to dismiss as New Age nonsense what Kenton says about the quality of love. But love isn't just something we make up. It's a real, physical and evolutionary force. Professor Leo Buscaglia, author of the international best seller *Living, Loving and Learning*, believes that love is crucial to our spiritual development. He writes,

> It's not enough to have lived. We should be determined to live for something. May I suggest that it be creating joy for others, sharing what we have for the betterment of personkind, bringing hope to the lost and love to the lonely.

In an interview just before he died, Buscaglia added importantly that 'love takes patience, knowledge, experience, determination and every positive trait we possess'.

Marianne Williamson, author of the wonderful *Return to Love*, believes that our ability to love helps us to connect with a deep inner knowing and a guiding wisdom:

> Something amazing happens when we surrender and just love. We melt into another world. A realm of power already within us. The world changes when we change. The world softens when we soften. The world loves us when we choose to love the world.
>
> Surrender means the decision to stop fighting the world, and to start loving it instead. It is a gentle liberation from pain. But liberation isn't about breaking out of anything; it's a gentle melting into who we really are.

The process of liberation

Many women I spoke to said that when they finally accepted that they had moved into a different phase of life, they felt a sense of liberation. An example is 54-year-old Sally, who before we spoke had never told anyone about the grief she was feeling about the menopause. On the surface, Sally was all smiles. Underneath, she felt isolated and angry. It was only when she came on one of my Sex, Meaning and Menopause workshops and shared her experiences with other women that she started to accept what was happening to her.

> I hadn't been able to close the chapter and get on with living this new life. The workshop helped me to do just that. I realized I *was* a postmenopausal woman, and no longer in that transition phase. It was time to say goodbye to the past. I found that very releasing. I'm now waiting to find how meaning will develop for me.

Even for those women who, unusually in my experience, *do* prepare themselves consciously for the menopause, there can still be surprises in store. Elizabeth had been determined to go through the menopause with as little upheaval as possible. So she read numerous books and went regularly to therapy. However, she realized she still wasn't happy with something she couldn't quite put her finger on. This feeling of unease began to grow. It was only when her therapist asked how her mother had experienced the menopause that she realized she connected the menopause with death. This helped her to release the grief and confusion she had been holding onto for years.

My mother went through the menopause and immediately got breast cancer. Although she carried on living for a further 17 years, she was horribly disfigured by the surgery she went through. Talking about her made me suddenly realize that I was waiting to get breast cancer too. It was such a powerful realization that I had to stop on my way home from the session and have some time to process it before I went back to my husband and children.

I now understand that although I take after my mother physically, I'm not like her at all. Her father died when she was six weeks old, and she carried this deep wounding all her life. She didn't 'do' emotions, and couldn't understand when any of her children did. So I was never encouraged to feel.

But that's totally against my nature. Seeing this clearly really helped me to separate from my mother's grief. It was a huge relief and release.

For Elizabeth, the menopause brought a profound shift in awareness.

It gave me the opportunity to sort things out, and to make these profound connections so I could move on in a different way. It's only then that you can look at what you're left with, and what you want to make of your life as you grow older.

As with significant personal growth at any time of life, finding one's inward truth and essence can have considerable consequences in the external world of relationships and friendships, work and position in society. One woman who experienced a feeling of 'coming home' as she went through the menopause realized that she was fed up with looking after her husband, who she experienced now as acting more like a child than a fellow 50-something-year-old. So she left him. Gail also felt the need to leave her 35-year marriage.

I'd brought up three children. My marriage had never been that good, and I felt it was time for a radical change. The decision to divorce was very frightening, but I knew I had to do it now or it would be too late. I haven't regretted it, though of course, such a massive life change at this stage of my life has had its own challenges. But these have forced me to become much wiser about life.

Some women, such as Nina who talked about her loss of libido in Chapter 3, discovered a new inner strength that had been absent before.

> The menopause has been the most phenomenal period of my life. I reached 50 and decided I was going to do a postgraduate degree. I would never have had the self-belief to do something like that before.
>
> It's almost like I turned my back on that part of myself which had stopped me from being who I really was. It was also the part that used to make me feel guilty, and drove me to behave in ways that made me lose respect for myself. Now I have a new sense of self-respect. My life is in far better shape and I like myself far better. I also like what I do because I've found meaning and purpose for my life through a charity I work for.

For many of us, as for me, the menopause also coincides with the time when our parents begin to die, or certainly can't be the parents they were. Caring for her ailing mother has helped Andrea to accept her own mortality and to understand her place in life.

> When my mother died it made me realize I was no longer young. I had become the older generation that she had always been to me. In the past, death felt as if it was far off in the future, but watching her die made me realize it was coming my way too.
>
> At the same time, my daughter left home, so I was forced to accept that my ageing process is part of the natural cycles of life. You have to stand aside for the younger generation to make their splash, just as my mother did for me.

Marianne was diagnosed with breast cancer shortly after her children left home. She has fully recovered and now, in her 60s, she was very aware that life is precious and short.

> I've never managed to get used to the fact the children don't live with us any more. But, I know I am lucky to be alive, and I want to make the most of every day I have. Even so, I am aware a whole day can go past, and I've done little else than walk the dog. Then again, I don't want to just fill up my life for the sake of it. I used to be a special needs teacher, and although rewarding, it was also exhausting.

I know how lucky I am with my marriage too. We've been together for over 35 years, and we make a point of going on a special date every week. I love spending time with my husband. But I am aware that I think about death a lot more these days. Having faced it as a younger woman, I often wonder how I will die as an old woman. I do *not* want to end up bent over or suffering from Alzheimer's. It also makes me wonder if I should be doing something more with my life while I can. But I know secretly I am waiting for my daughter to have her first child. I want to be available to help and support her in any way I can.

Many other women also spoke about the joys of grandparenting, and how it gave them new meaning and purpose. Liza has several grandchildren.

Sex is not part of how I find meaning any more – certainly not like it used to be. My family and being a granny have become much more important. It's so exciting to watch my grandchildren grow up.

These days I have a lot more time to enjoy everything and I make meaning for myself in the things I choose to do. Apart from my grandchildren, I have a large circle of friends who are very important to me, and I work in a community project which gives me a lot of purpose.

For Amy, supporting her daughter and grandchildren had become the most important thing in her life, although in ways she hadn't expected.

My retirement isn't what I thought it was going to be. One of my grandchildren has a severe congenital illness which means she can't walk, and it's possible that the younger child might have it too. My husband and I spend a lot of time helping my daughter, and we are very active in raising sponsorship for new research. Once these new drugs have been developed, it will make a huge difference to my granddaughter.

Even though I have no other ambition but to help, I am clear that my role is supporter, not main carer. I want to be a grandmother, not a mother. I've done all that. Anyway, my husband and I need time together. We enjoy each other's company and we're both fit and healthy, so we spend a lot of time walking when we're not looking after the grandchildren. We love that.

Listening to women talking about how they have made meaning in their lives brought home to me just how individual a process this is. For some, like the two women earlier who spoke about their anger, it's been like a baptism of fire. For some, such as Elizabeth who made such a powerful connection between her growing unease and her mother's breast cancer, it's been about profound personal insights. For others, like the last two grandmothers we heard from, it's been more a gentle transition, but no less extraordinary.

Sex and spirituality

These individual stories of personal meaning, often in the smaller and private experiences of family and relationship, reminded me of Mother Theresa's comment that 'There are no great deeds – just small deeds done with great love.'

And in that context, I began to ask myself how menopausal and postmenopausal sex, with all its complexities, fits in with those themes of spirituality and love. Are they compatible? I empathized with one interviewee who said, 'I've had quite enough sex in my life, thank you very much. I know what it's like, and it's much more important for me to concentrate on my spiritual development. But I rarely tell anyone I feel like this because when I have, they've looked at me as if I'm mad.'

But, why – especially when we're more mature – it is such an embarrassment to admit publicly that you would rather put your energy into spiritual development than have sex?

Sex and sin

To make sense of these connections, it's useful to consider how the conflict between sex and spirituality has evolved over the centuries in Western society. It seems to me to go a very long way back into the roots of our Judaeo-Christian culture, to concepts of original sin, to the Psalms and to Genesis and the Old Testament story of Adam and Eve.

So, if you will bear with me for the next page or so, I'll start in the beginning, as it were, in the Garden of Eden. God seemed to be quite happy for Adam and Eve to enjoy sex: 'Be fruitful,' he told them, 'and increase in number.' The problem arose when Eve tempted Adam to disobey God's instructions not to eat from the tree of knowledge, and got them both expelled from the garden for their defiance.

This 'new' confusion around sin and sex became both personal and doctrinal with the Psalms of David, most famously in Psalm 51, the text of which is perhaps best known from the magical, high-soaring seventeenth-century setting by Allegri.

> Have mercy upon me, O God, *[writes David]* according to thy lovingkindness: according unto the multitude of thy tender mercies blot out my transgressions.
> Wash me throughly from mine iniquity, and cleanse me from my sin.
> For I acknowledge my transgressions: and my sin is ever before me.
> Against thee, thee only, have I sinned, and done this evil in thy sight: that thou mightest be justified when thou speakest, and be clear when thou judgest.
> Behold, I was shapen in iniquity; and in sin did my mother conceive me.

Forgive the brief biblical excursion; this really matters, for it seems to me that it's that last line that did the damage. And it's worth repeating: *in sin did my mother conceive me.*

It sounds to be declaring that the very act of sex itself, and of conception, is in some way originally sinful. So, for some 3,000 years during which the Old Testament has been considered to be the absolute word of God, there's been a confusion about sex at the very heart of Judaeo-Christian tradition and morality. (What's often forgotten in the dogma, of course, is that David's psalm was a very personal guilty plea to God for forgiveness for having raped Bathsheba, to whom King David had taken a fancy.)

This struggle between sin and sex certainly caused St Augustine of Hippo considerable trouble in the fifth century AD, as Christianity was beginning to take a hold across the Europe of the Roman Empire. Augustine was a Roman from North Africa, born in 430AD, who became one of the most important figures in the development of Western Christianity. His teachings on salvation and divine grace profoundly influenced the medieval world view, but St Augustine's struggle to overcome his sexual desires and fantasies caused him anguish throughout his life. Ultimately, he came to the conclusion that there is a part of us which predates our development of mental and spiritual control. He called this wild, untameable part 'original sin' – echoing David's interpretation of being sinful from the very moment of conception. Augustine finally concluded that the sacred bond of marriage between a man and a woman, blessed by God, was the only way that sex could be acceptable – but not for fun, only for procreation.

Today, even if we still enjoy the singing of Psalm 51, we've at last moved on a bit. Science has confirmed how sex and physical touch play a central role in our desire for intimacy, and how we find safety and meaning in the world through our attachments with other fellow humans. For example, physical, loving contact between mother and baby is critical to the way we learn to feel good about ourselves as we grow up. At the same time, we also now understand sexual desire as a natural biological urge to reproduce as well as being a sensual pleasure, and certainly not to be something that is regarded as 'sinful'.

Catholic priests may still be required to commit to celibacy (an idea, of course, that took root in the Church only a full millennium after Christ, who never suggested the idea). But sex has thankfully ceased to be shackled to religious dogma, and with the sexual revolution of the 1960s, we have been given permission to enjoy it as much as we want.

Even so, being brought up by the Second World War generation who still looked to the Church for moral guidance, sex for many baby boomers has never quite lost that 'naughty' edge. This makes it hard to talk about, and confusing when society sensationalizes those who continue to have sex, and scoffs at those who don't want to.

'The perspective isn't right,' says legendary agony aunt Virginia Ironside. 'Of course,' she told me, 'some of us want to remain sexual until a great age, but who cares. It doesn't matter. The sooner people realize there's nothing wrong with having sex, or not having sex, we can relax.'

Before I climb off this particular soapbox, I want to say that even if the Church, in my view, got the physicality of sex spectacularly wrong, there *is* something profoundly sacred about sexual union, reflected also in the teachings of esoteric traditions, for example in Buddhism. It throws a very different light on the way perfunctory sex can be very disappointing, and even shaming.

Those who practise the ancient art of tantric sex, such as the couple we heard from in Chapter 3, say that without a deep spiritual understanding of how sexual intercourse helps us to unite with higher aspects of ourselves, sex for its own sake is unfulfilling, and also destructive to the spirit.

According to Hindu scriptures, tantric sexuality is one dimension of a spiritual path that is devoted to the supreme search for the self: the godhead. Sacred sexual union between man and woman is said to release what the Hindus and Buddhists call the Kundalini energy – a combined spiritual and sexual force latent within every human being – taking them beyond orgasm to reach the ecstatic states of the godhead itself.

Many psychologists in the West have studied Kundalini energy. Carl Jung compared its power to that of the libido, and William Reich, a psychoanalyst in the 1930s, recognized sexuality as the primary life force, giving it the name Orgone energy. More recently, Thomas Moore, the American Christian theologian and therapist, has written extensively on spirituality and sexuality. He believes the act of making love is a 'soul-making' opus. In *Dark Nights of the Soul*, he says that no matter how negative the sexual experience, it has the potential to do 'nothing less than make you into a person and to create a world that is sensuous and alive.'

Going beyond sex

When sex is described like that it's difficult to imagine why anyone would want to give up this intimate way of nurturing ourselves and each other. But during my own menopause, something more changed than just the physiological shutting down of my ovaries. It felt as if I didn't need sex any more to feel sensuous and alive. In fact, as the years have gone by, I have been surprised to feel more alive, productive and feminine than I did as a sexually active woman.

The Reverend Kachinas Kutenai, an Apache medicine woman, talks about menopause as a time when a woman can finally put sex into its proper perspective. 'You don't need an orgasm to smile and your conversation is no longer sex-filled,' she says in *Red Moon Passage*. She continues, 'When you stop being dominated by sexuality, when you stop being controlled by it, you view things differently. This is part of the change that happens naturally as you grow older – if we let it, that is.'

This change of view is not just a female prerogative. At the age of 70, the fourth century BC Greek playwright Sophocles replied to the question whether he still had sex: 'Hush, man; most gladly indeed am I rid of it all, as though I had escaped from a mad and savage master.' And he wasn't talking about his wife.

I know there are plenty of women and men who continue to enjoy sex as part of their personal development, and that there are also those who choose celibacy as part of their spiritual discipline. But there is a difference between the choice not to be sexual when the body wants it, and libido naturally fading as part of the ageing process.

Iris, now postmenopausal and unbothered by sex, is a former member of a religious group that had strict celibacy rules. She explained how she experienced the difference between abstaining from sex and the sexual changes she went through during the menopause.

> It's a completely different experience from choosing to be celibate. I gave up sex in my 40s when I joined the group. At the time I was married, and, of course, the marriage folded because of this.
>
> Eventually I left the group because I started to want sex a lot. I looked for a man as soon as possible and went a bit wild. I can remember feeling how strange it was to be going mad like this in my late 40s, but I didn't think of myself as old. I still don't. It's just that my body is reacting differently now I have been through the menopause. I have no craving for sex like that any more.

I asked Iris if she missed sex, or envied other women who continued to enjoy it. 'How can you envy something that you don't want any more?' she asked. 'You can in your head, I suppose, but not in your body.' I resonate with this. I can still think about sex quite happily, and even imagine having sex. But because I don't have the hormones any more, my body doesn't react, and there's no feeling of distress – until that is, I think of my dear old husband.

Using ritual

One way of caring for ourselves and our souls at the time of menopause is to turn this into a sacred experience, and to ritualize the transition.

Since humans first began to walk upright, ritual has been used to mark the transition from one state of being to another: baptism, confirmation, marriage and funerals, to name four that we use in our society today. These rites of passage encourage us to identify and accept that something has changed in the person's life, and a new respect is granted.

Some women I know are beginning to use home-grown rituals to celebrate their rite of passage into elder stateswomen, witnessed by their close friends. For example, one friend held a 'croning' ceremony to combine the celebration of her sixtieth birthday with her passage into being postmenopause. It was a wonderfully joyous affair, full of flowers, poetry and poignant quotations from wise women friends. Between us, we created a web of the world by entwining string between us, onto which we tied mementoes and crystals. A sumptuous and fun-filled lunch helped to further honour the experience.

Another friend has a more personal and private relationship with her menopause, seeing it as a shamanic journey which she told me was helping her to 'go down into the pit of the earth to be dismembered, and then at some point returning to the surface of the earth in a new form.' She was conscious of this process every day. She added that she would know intuitively when her shamanic journeying is complete, and would then decide how to celebrate it.

For myself, I chose to recognize that I was moving into my postmenopausal years by going on an eight-day silent Ignatian retreat in North Wales. I wanted to spend time thinking about my ageing process, my fading sexuality and what it means to become an older member of society. It's one thing to talk about the menopause, or even write about it. It's another to sit with it, and meet it. What can I offer now? How can I offer what I have?

I may not be a religious person in the sense of the established Church, but I do have a strong faith (a mishmash of Christianity, Buddhism, Sufism, Hinduism, plus other religious and spiritual beliefs I've met along the way) that has helped me to develop my own understanding of the divine masculine and feminine. I suppose some would call it paganism; others might think it New Age, perhaps mysticism. But when it comes to faith, I don't like labels. It's too personal, and who's to say one belief is better than another? All I know is that I have a faith in something far greater than me. Without it, I would be lost. It was with some trepidation that I owned up to this at my first retreat session with Maggie, my Spiritual Director and a Catholic ex-nun.

Maggie was truly wonderful: non-judgemental, open, compassionate, kind and very human, the archetypal wise woman who had embraced her own ageing process. During our daily half-hour meetings, Maggie allowed me to struggle with all kinds of troubles and doubts. To help me connect more deeply with the sacred feminine, she introduced me to *Soul Sisters: Women in Scripture Speak to Women Today*, a collection of poems by the American author Edwina Gateley, beautifully illustrated with portraits by Louis

Glanzman. This extract particularly resonated with me, and is from the poem dedicated to Anna the Prophetess:

> Your wisdom, Anna
> revealed to you
> the deeper truths
> from which we hide
> when we deny
> the beauty and significance of old age.
> Anna, sister, Prophetess,
> speaker of the truth,
> help us to reclaim
> that we which we have left behind –
> our woman's gifts – abandoned,
> our journey aborted and denied
> in our sad efforts
> to hide
> from all that we could be.

When Maggie sent me off to visit holy wells in the area, now over-grown nature havens, I felt as if Anna the Prophetess had climbed into the car beside me. Having the time to sit beside these pools and reflect quietly on what was important gave me a greater perspective on life, and an enjoyable sense that I was at last beginning to know myself as an older woman.

Caroline Born, a dancer and choreographer, decided to create a dance performance to ritualize her menopause, which she also made into a film called *From the Red to the Silver*. She told me,

> Menopause is such an important time in a woman's life, and I believe we need to honour it.
>
> The filming took place on the beach in Devon because I wanted an archetypal link between women and nature. There were two groups of dancers, one group still menstruating, the other had 'silver hair.'
>
> Those women still menstruating danced on the red sandstone rocks, while those who were postmenopausal danced at the edge of the silver waves. I moved between each group of dancers, neither in one place or the other. I am not menstruating, but I am not old. So who am I? What am I? So, for me, menopause is about allowing my spiritual side to come alive.

Wisdom from the silver-haired

We've heard how important spiritual development is for many women reaching the menopause. For some, the loss of libido allows them to enter into a deeper understanding of themselves, and what they want to do with their lives. For this final section, I interviewed several women in their 60s who were a little further along on their journey. I found their wisdom, humility and humour truly inspiring.

Veronica is the managing director of a human resources company. For her, growing older had helped her to appreciate that everyone has a story to tell.

> I was in a real muddle when I reached 60, but being on this side of the menopause is fantastic. Okay, I hate seeing my reflection, but I've always been like that since I was a child. You have to laugh, and remember not to put yourself in front of mirrors or bright lights.
>
> Every day is such an incredible challenge. It's the whole bit of knowing less and less about everything because you actually know so much. I find that so fresh and exciting. You see people in a different way too. I'm always looking at their faces and wondering what stories are written in those wrinkles? It's fascinating. As a young person you don't notice because you're too busy chasing your tail. I like standing back, stepping out of the game, and becoming the watcher. It gives me such a rich life.
>
> Actually, I finally feel I've arrived. I'm not afraid of anyone or intimidated by what they do or what they represent. I know I'm going to ashes one day, and so are they. I find that liberating.

Amanda is 65 and a writer.

> When I look at photographs of myself at 48 and now, I have to face the truth that my ageing process has been phenomenal. But I'm also in a completely different mindset. I feel like I'm living as I want to.
>
> Okay, I would be lying if I said I don't care about my looks, but loss is all part of the process of growing older, especially for women. It's not like the terrible grief of someone you love dying. It's different, and can be a fantastic, liberating experience, if you choose to embrace it. Anyway, we all have to go through it. It's part of the deal of becoming who you are as an older woman.
>
> My spiritual beliefs have deepened, and helped to put life into

perspective. It allows me to let go and watch things unfold in their own time – life is bigger than me, and I need to remember that.

Barbara is 69 and, not one to sit back and wait for the end, she recently trained as a dance therapist.

What do I remember about my menopause? I must have been in my early 50s. That would be around the time my husband got a 20-year-old girl pregnant, brought her home and asked what 'we' could do about it. I was on the brink of what I thought was the ideal life, and Wham! I ended up with no home, £37 in the bank, and a beaten-up Mini. That was tough, but I managed. You do manage. You have to.

I ended up working as a carer in Wales, and from there I started again. Now I look back on those days and shrug. When you are thrown into a situation like I was, you have to learn to trust. Sometimes it's the only thing left to do. I threw myself into my new life and got on with it. It was very tough financially for a while but it helped when I inherited my dad's house after he died. I now have just about enough, what with my pension, and it means I can afford to pay for my dance classes.

I have found profound meaning in my life through Biodanza (also known as the 'Dance of Life'). It's about learning to connect and express wellbeing through movement. It's helped me to heal, and to find out who I am, and who I want to become. I find that very exciting at the age of 69.

I can also look back on my life and see where I've come from – I know lies and violence, and believe me, I gave as good as I got. Now I see the importance of connection, of understanding the importance of taking hold of someone's elbow when they are in distress and saying, 'There's more going on here than you realize.' It's not about setting yourself up as a teacher, but helping people to tap into their real selves. That's where their answers lie, no matter how awful it is on the outside.

If I were to give advice to a woman in her 50s, I would tell her to give up trying to control what's happening. Just trust your instinct and your heart. They will lead you in the right direction. But I also realize that you can only say this to someone who is ready to hear it. The other thing I would say is that getting older may not be about orgasmic thrills any more, but that doesn't mean to say you can't feel sensual and deeply in touch with the feminine. Our mothers never had this opportunity. We do, so make the most of it.

As a woman approaching 70, I see my task as helping younger women to know that life is rather like a game, and how they develop their own rules to make it work for them. It's up to all of us to be as creative and inspiring as we can be so we can get back in touch with the mystery of nature and what it gives us.

Pauline is a 64-year-old artist, and is in a gay relationship.

I think that growing into an older woman, whether you are straight or gay, is about learning to discern between love and sex. There's the entanglement of love and sex and there's an integrated understanding of what the two are. When you know the difference, it gives you a sense of peace.

I find purpose in my life by learning to accept and live with my shortcomings, and doing the same with Sandra, my partner. I am learning that it's okay to have humdinging rows. We carry on loving each other even when we don't like each other in the moment. It's about plastering on a whole deeper meaning of how we live together. This is overlaid by an increasing awareness that time is short. I don't mean that morosely. Rather it gives us permission to do things while we still can. That's our excuse to travel a lot!

Natalie is an American photographer who now lives in the UK.

Looking back on my younger self, I feel compassion towards her for believing she could get love through sex. That was her sum value. If you share yourself intimately with someone, it's not about having a good fuck. It's about sharing your soul, your dreams, your family. For example, seeing my partner with my son and his family touches a deep place in me.

I have friends of my age who talk about how great their sex life still is. But what are they *really* trying to say? Why do they need to say it anyway? I don't need to know how sexual they are. I would rather know how they feel about each other and if they're happy together. Saying you have sex doesn't demonstrate how much you love someone. Loving someone is a state of being, and there's a lot more to it than banging away at each other. That kind of sex doesn't last long anyway, not when you get to my age.

I'm not at all upset about being postmenopausal. I like maturing. It doesn't make me any less of a woman or a person to have reached this stage in my life. I like seeing everything differently, and I like how my values have changed. I don't care about pleasing people all the time, or what I am supposed to be in other people's interpretation. I am alright as I am.

Fiona is in her mid-60s.

It's only when you look back on the menopause that you realize how much has changed. I was in my early 40s when I went through it. I was living in a house with a load of teenagers and a very rocky marriage. I was also holding down a high-powered job and jetting off around the world. I don't really remember those years, apart from them being very busy.

My life changed drastically when my husband retired. I gave up work and we sold everything. I also gave up alcohol and cigarettes, had a hysterectomy and then we ended up living on a narrowboat. We stopped doing that when my husband couldn't manage any more because of ill health. I was his carer for years.

I've been on my own for quite a while now. It took a bit of getting used to, but I enjoy it. I also like being older. I've come to terms with it. It's okay to look at my body and see that I'm different. I'm often told I look younger than I am, which is nice. But what's important is having 65 years of life experience under my belt. That's what I trade on.

What would I say to a woman approaching 50? You need to know that the menopause will pass and that the need for sex will pass. But you will need to find meaning for yourself and to know who you are. It's nothing to do with a formula; it's about developing and learning to trust your intuition. It's such a great feeling when you get it.

For me, one of the most inspirational postmenopausal women today is 82-year-old Myrrha Stanford-Smith, who at the time of writing has just had her first novel *The Great Lie* published. She has been given a three-book deal by her publisher. I hope I'll still be equally engaged with life at her age.

Until now, this book has focused on women's experience of the menopause. In the next chapter we hear what it's like from the male perspective. Some readers may be very surprised.

CHAPTER 5

Men talking about the menopause

I was brought up by a father who was unable and unwilling to express his emotions. So I grew up believing that men were emotional cripples. I now know this isn't true (most of the time), but it took me years to appreciate that when it comes to life, love and loss, men in their different ways suffer just as much as we women do. The main difference, perhaps, is that we women have each other to moan to, or to pick up the pieces when our worlds have fallen apart. Men don't have that innate capacity. They may mumble to their mates over a pint about something that's bothering them, but it's rarely an open or honest conversation. From what I've heard, when it gets anywhere near the knuckle, especially when sex isn't so great, the discussion normally dissolves into something along the lines of footballs scores, derailleur gears, some fatuous comment about tits, or which celebrity has taken pole position for the fastest car lap on *Top Gear*.

So it was with some apprehension that I started to inquire, through friends and female interviewees, if they knew of husbands and partners who would be willing to talk about their experiences of the menopause. I was amazed when the nine men whose stories form this chapter stepped forward. They were more than eager to tell me their stories. Most of them, like the man I met at the Christmas party in the beginning of the book, who said he'd be happier putting his head in snake pit than talking to his wife about sex, had never spoken about these things to anyone. So I feel honoured that they chose to open up to me. It may have helped that I did not know most of them, and conducted all but two interviews on the telephone. Perhaps hearing a genuinely interested but disembodied voice made it easier for them to say what they truly felt.

No matter, these men certainly brought home to me that not *all* men of a certain age go daft in the head, or run off with younger women. Admittedly, some were in second and third marriages. Some were struggling with a lack of sex. Some had strayed and come back.

Some had found their menopausal wives unpredictable and difficult to live with. But quite clearly, these men were not just fond of their wives and partners, but also willing to find ways of working through the menopausal changes that their relationships were undergoing.

Hearing them talk so eloquently about such private, intimate matters, reminded me of a comment made by the American writer Henry Thoreau:

> The greatest compliment that was ever paid to me was when someone asked me what I thought, and attended my answer.

So, sometimes being guilty of not being fully attentive to the man with whom I share my life, I take a step back in this section to allow the men to speak for themselves.

Although some of the men mention similar issues, each one offers a different view. Ray talks of his despair at no longer having a satisfying sex life. Brian has an open relationship, although he's aware this will change as he and his wife grow older. Chris is frustrated with the lack of information available for men married to menopausal women. David recognizes how the menopause can widen cracks that already exist in the relationship. Nick uses pornography to compensate for the lack of sex. Will is the one in the partnership with low libido. Gary talks about an affair he had when his wife was going through the menopause. John looks at the menopause as a natural progression to wisdom. Finally, Daniel suggests that men and women are indeed from different planets.

My hope is their voices will help couples to talk more openly with each other about the menopause. I also think some women might be astonished to learn exactly how much does go on behind that raised newspaper.

Ray, 62 – The word I use is despair

> We married one year before she started the menopause. That was ten years ago. To be honest, she's no longer the same woman. She became irritable and angry and lost direction, which I found very confusing. When I look back to the horny little thing I met, I wonder where the excitement's gone. It's not that sex has totally disappeared, but that wonderful edge – that sexual tension – is no longer there. That's certainly not what I bargained for.
>
> Sex has always been the driving force in my life. It gave rise to all

sorts of creativity and formed a big part of that risk to be intimate. Without it, I know I'm much more distant. I wasn't brought up to be intimate. I had to learn how as I grew up. So it's been very difficult to watch this intimacy fade away again. I need sex for those moments of intense connection.

The word I would use is despair. It's the recognition that at the age of 62 I've had the best of my sex life. I don't feel ready to give it up, but I don't want to give up my marriage either. Not at my age. Yes, I know esoteric teachers talk about rising higher than sexual desire in order to meet God. But for me, that's a load of bollocks.

Because of the lack of sex, I've found it difficult to keep my feelings for my wife alive. It comes out in the way I tease her. I probably do it far more than is good for either of us. Sometimes it's funny, but I know that when it's day in, day out, it wears her down. I've realized that going away together helps. But that only happens about three times a year. And this lubrication business isn't very sexy. We have to take a ruddy great haversack full of lubricants and what-have-you.

There's nothing more exciting for me than being with a woman who's dripping wet. It's so animal. She might have a spectacular orgasm, which leaves me with this great feeling that I have achieved something in my life. I know that sounds daft, but it's the truth. So, when you have to pile on – or in – these blasted lubricants, it takes the edge off it – and boy, do you have to keep a sense of humour.

I have no problem with my wife's body, or the fact she's ageing. So am I. In fact, I love the way she looks. She's still a beautiful woman to me. But I get confused when she wants to get close to me because closeness in the past has always led to sex. So I tend to step onto the practical level to avoid it. This means I've got out of the habit of having sex with her.

I want it with other women I meet though, and I've had to make very clear boundaries for myself. I also dream about it a lot. It's always very erotic – with some kind of exchange of juices. Yet, even in these dreams I know it's wrong because there's something in the background telling me not to go any further. It's hard for me. I mean, for heaven's sake, making love makes me feel alive, adoring and cherishing. I can go out and serve my partner in all sorts of different ways. But now it's like, well, here's Saturday to tick things off on the 'to do' list.

It's very personal to talk like this, and I can feel a sense of relief for putting it into words. My male friends laugh about the lack of sex, but we don't talk about it in any depth. More like, 'So, did you get any this weekend?' The bloke usually shakes his head and has another beer.

My wife and I do, sort of, talk about what's changing. The last conversation was about my need to spend more time with my male friends, or doing things outside the home on my own, like fishing or playing music in a band. I'm aware that she agrees to this on one level, but then finds ways of stopping me on the other. Perhaps I need to make it clearer that I'm not going anywhere else. I value what we have too much.

I make meaning in my life through my work. Does it compensate for lack of sex? Not even close. When I was younger, sex and meaning were conjoined. Now it's looking round to see if someone wants help to cross the street, or picking up litter that's ruining a beautiful view.

I think a lot of men share this grief, particularly younger men in their mid-40s whose partners don't want it any more. Men are driven by sex and defined by it, and none of us has any idea what we are heading into while rampaging through our 20s and 30s. The big rip-off is living with a fantasy that women are gagging for sex. It's simply not true. Okay, maybe for a short time while they are looking for a mate to reproduce with. Once that's been done, the male needs to go off and tear up fields with his antlers. But this isn't allowed. We're expected to settle down and trim hedges.

I think women fare much better as they age. My wife is like an old mother bear who knows what she wants. She's gone down to her boots, if you like. She's powerful and clear and fearless these days. So, you see, I have a humdinger of a woman who loves life, but doesn't want sex.

Brian, 53 – We've always had an open relationship

My wife went through the menopause in her late 40s. I haven't noticed much change in her sexually. She's a very attractive and sexy woman, and yes, there are still times when I still fancy her. But it's not often.

We've been through quite a few difficult patches over the past 30-odd years we've been together. It's stopped me feeling any real desire for her. Actually, we both feel the same, which is why we both have affairs.

We've always had an open relationship, mainly because I don't

believe in monogamy. I know this sounds strange because of the
length of time we've been together. But we met when we were very
young, and in a way, we've grown used to each other's foibles.

I've never felt threatened by the thought of my wife leaving
me for someone else, but I have felt jealous about some of the
relationships she's been in. I think that's a natural reaction for most
males. Women look for strong genes to mate with. But I'm not sure
what happens when the menopause arrives. Do women still look for
that in men?

My experience of some postmenopausal women is that they're
comfortable with what's happening to them, and they remain just as
highly sexed. My wife's certainly like that, but I've noticed that a few
of her friends who've been through the menopause seem to have
changed in that department. The fact she hasn't changed means she's
still sexually confident, and I think that really helps her. She looks at
least 10 years younger than most of her peer group, and I know she's
not on HRT. At the same time I've noticed that she's less confident
about the way she thinks about herself, but I put that down to the
very difficult childhood she had. It's had a massive impact on her life,
and perhaps this is also why I have never left.

Sometimes I tell her about my relationships. Since we've both had
affairs, it's easier. But we don't talk that much about it. She's always
been more open than me, and it's comforting for me to know she has
a lover. It wouldn't be fair otherwise – as long as it doesn't threaten
what we have. Ten years ago I got badly bitten. The relationship
went much further than it should have and a lot of people got
unnecessarily hurt. So I'm very cautious these days – if someone's
getting too keen I back off, and I'm also cautious about what I
actually say to my wife. I've never found her very good at listening,
and that's always been a problem.

Looking back, I realize that I married far too young. I was 19 at
the time. We met abroad, and both of us were living from day to
day without much of a plan. So we drifted into the relationship and
within a few months she was pregnant with our first child. It was
very difficult, because I already knew our relationship wasn't right,
but I lacked the courage to end it. In truth, it's always been like that.
I was finally getting to the point of leaving when she fell pregnant
with our youngest daughter. Even though my wife was only in her
mid-40s, she thought she was menopausal, so she stopped taking
contraception. Personally, I've always been rather suspicious about
that. Anyway, it certainly stopped me from leaving. I'm glad now,

because I would have hated for my daughter – she's coming up to 13 – to have come from a broken home.

Now I'm in my 50s, I have much more awareness about how life works, although I don't think much about spirituality, or stuff like that. I don't believe there's any more to life than what's in front of your nose. But sometimes I look at my wife and think about the huge life we've had together. Neither of us are the same person we were when we married. Actually, I realize that the older she becomes, the more protective I feel about her, which is strange given how difficult our relationship has been.

As I grow older I can imagine staying with my wife but continuing to have lovers. I can see us hobbling around on our walking frames together, and obviously I'd be more monogamous. Well, the opportunities dry up with age. I assume it will with her too.

I rarely – if ever – talk to other men about their wives going through the menopause. Sometimes I've spoken to my wife about it, and that's helped when things have become fraught. But that only happens a couple of times a year. Occasionally I talk to one of my girlfriends. Some have been older than me. I find older women just as attractive as long as they keep themselves fit and trim. It's not great if they let their bodies go, but the most important thing – more important than sex – is intelligence. Without exception all my lovers have had degrees. My wife is very creative in lots of ways but she never went to university, and she's not the type to go now she's older.

David, 59 – Menopause highlights the cracks already there

I've been married three times. My first wife and I were too young. We met at university, and although we got on really well – and still do – it wasn't great sexually. Even though we had two children, neither of us was prepared to put up with it, and I'd been playing around a bit, so we broke up.

I met my second wife while I working abroad. We were married for 18 years, and to be honest it was always difficult. We almost split up a couple of times, but I didn't want to put our two children through it, not after the first time.

When we did finally come to grief, I wasn't aware of her being menopausal. Perhaps that was part of the problem. She was certainly having hot flushes, and didn't want sex. Actually, she didn't want to be touched at all. Before that, she had been vigorously sexual,

so it was difficult to accept what had changed. I know she was
having irregular periods, but there wasn't a possibility of her getting
pregnant because I'd had a vasectomy by then. This also could have
been a problem. She wanted to have more children, and now I
realize she was in the process of facing the fact she would never
have another one. She was very sensitive about this. Looking back, of
course, I can see she was going through the menopause. But it was,
for me anyway, a gradual process and I didn't really understand what
was going on.

Sex has always been really important to me, but I went along with
everything for a while, making do. For most guys who don't have sex,
there are three options: don't do anything, masturbate, or go with
another woman. I chose the middle option because I'd already been
down the 'other woman' route. I knew this time there was too much
at stake. I kept telling myself that for a long time.

Of course it's more complicated than saying we broke up because
of not having sex. Really, we reached a stage where we had grown
apart. Classic, I suppose. In the past, sex was the glue that bound us
together. It helped us to feel warm towards each other. When that
went, well, you're just thrown back on your differences. Added to
which, our children were reaching adolescence so I was very aware
of sex at the other end of spectrum. I felt like I was dropping off the
end of the conveyer belt, which I wasn't ready for.

I also started to feel very marginalized, especially when we ended
up in separate bedrooms. I was servicing the family financially, eating
with them, playing with them, and driving them around – being part
of family life without have a relationship with my wife. It made me
feel lonely, sad and angry. To compensate, I would write books, think
a lot and enjoy my work – it's not difficult to get drawn into different
things – and I did occasionally talk to a couple of male friends in the
sense of 'not getting it.' I remember one saying, 'Well, that's how it
can be.'

But, you know, putting it crudely, there's only so long you want to
wank. Eventually I became involved with a woman I had met several
years earlier. We were both very attracted to each other at the
time, but neither of us wanted to take it any further because of our
marriages and children. When she finally decided to get divorced she
called me up. And that was it.

I am very happy with my third wife. It's a completely different
relationship to anything I have experienced before. But I still bitterly
regret breaking up with my second wife because of what it did to

the children. I know she and I would have been hard pushed to stay together in the long run, but I would have liked to have kept going until the kids were in their 20s. I'm sure we would have broken up then, but it would have been on a different basis, and had different consequences.

Talking about this, I can see how the menopause throws up cracks that are already there in the marriage. Unless there's a deep understanding between the two of you, it can be really difficult. Good communication is so important. Just the act of saying how sad, lonely, isolated, superfluous and marginalized you feel helps. The other person is usually feeling the same thing anyway. So perhaps, if you're both open, you may be able to find a new way of talking to each other again.

Having said that, I think your 50s are a major rain check. I was 55 when we broke up, and I can remember thinking, 'Christ, my dad died at 78. So that means for me, it's 20 more years and counting.' I have always sympathized with Henry Thoreau's lives of quiet desperation, but after thinking of my dad, I did not want to go gentle into that good night.

I'm still feeling battered by the divorce, and I'm still angry about what happened. But my new wife has introduced me to yoga, which has helped me to ground myself and to get a grip on my moods. Even though there's carnage in the background, I can see things are at last settling. So, yes, I'm alive. I am alive.

I have never felt good about having had affairs, but that's what happens when you don't have sex. So it's very important for men to understand the menopause, and really appreciate what happens to their wife. I was completely dense about it. I wanted to be comforting and supporting – but if you feel driven off, and realize your wife no longer wants to be your partner, it's very hard. I always say, with an edge to my voice, that my second wife was a wonderful mother. Full stop.

I would love to know how other couples have got through the menopause, particularly men. But we aren't given a voice in the way we experience what happens. I've certainly never spoken about it before. It's important to go deeper. We're living in a culture which has truncated our life experience. You're either young, or you fall into the image of being a sweet, dear old thing or some grumpy bastard. We aren't given time for the ageing process to mature in its own way, or to understanding how our 50s are such a time of transition. Before we reach our dotage, there are huge numbers of us having a quite a difficult time at this end of things. It needs to be recognized.

Chris, 52 – The media are hopeless when it comes to the menopause

I think we're pressurized by society to remain youthful, and that includes our sexual behaviour. Actually, it's pure fiction, whether you are young or old. The media fail to provide an actual portrayal of the ageing process. I get particularly narked by images of grey-haired couples, shown as fit, vibrant 70-year-olds sailing into the sunset. Nothing about what older people really need. The way youth are portrayed isn't much better. They always seem to be fighting over money or getting pissed. But when it comes to menopause it's very poor. If it's spoken about at all, it's about how older women can stay looking young, how they have bagged a mate half their age, or how they look fantastic after child number three. Not a word about what they think and feel about the menopause.

From what I can make out, women's magazines are particularly guilty. They have lots of articles about the menopause, but nothing of substance. Since we're living so much longer, it means we have another 20 years of sex to worry about, but there's very little information for blokes to know how to manage the sexual changes that their wives go through.

I've always been faithful to my wife, so the notion of sex is always tied up with her. Things are shifting though. She wakes up at night, soaked in sweat. It's been going on for the past six or seven months. It only happens at night, as far as I can tell, or that's what she says. It hasn't changed our relationship though – she's just as ratty as before!

I wanted to know about these hot sweats, so I trawled the internet. All I could understand is that the menopause is tied up with a system failure of some kind, which can end up with a hysterectomy. I was confused by that because it seemed to suggest that when you take out the ovaries, you are getting rid of the cause of the menopause. But someone I know has had a hysterectomy, and is still going through all the symptoms, and I've read virtually nothing about understanding how relationships can become quite difficult at this time of life.

I think there needs to be much more information available for those who want it. Of course you can't bombard children with this stuff. It's extraneous to their lives. But something should be there for them if they want to understand what's happening to their mum. For example, I had a notion of the menopause from my own mother. Occasionally, there would be sanitary towels in the bathroom, but she never discussed it. I didn't find out much more from an older woman I had an affair with. I was in my 20s at the time, and she was in her early 50s. I don't think she was menopausal because she certainly didn't have a problem with sex.

Actually, I would like more information about the whole matter of sex. Sex is important to me. It always has been, and I find it hard to maintain an equilibrium if I don't have it regularly. When my wife's ill, my first emotion is anxiety, and then fury that this might be time off sex. If she didn't want it any more, I'd find that hard. It's only recently that I've not needed to ejaculate twice a day. But, I think sex is much more important for men than it is for women, especially as we age. If she did ever say she didn't feel like it any more, I understand there are hormone treatments which could buy me ten more years of fucking, but it wouldn't do her much good. They have some pretty nasty side effects as far as I can make out. I certainly wouldn't insist she go on it. You can't insist another person takes medicine, but if I couldn't have sex I would go into a 20-year sulk. Of course, it would be different if she suffered an awful accident. I would still sulk, but with more dignity.

Mind you, I've always had a sexual fantasy going on. This has changed as I've grown older. Rather than focusing on a sex-kitten celebrity, I've invented an imaginary relationship with the celebrity's older cousin. This fantasy figure is about 49 and maturing naturally, the same as me. I find that very titillating. So for me it's not about going for sexual perfection any more. I think this is a normal reaction to my ageing process – a natural barrier to finding young women attractive and the vainglorious hope that they will want to have sex with me. That agenda is always running for men.

The fact that visions of beauty change over time is reflected in the mirror when I am standing next to my wife in the morning, brushing our teeth. Having said that, I seldom masturbate these days. This might be hormonal changes on my part, responding to what's happening to her. I don't know. But it's interesting that these days I can only get an erection when I'm with her. No-one else.

I would like to end by saying that as soon as your wife starts to have symptoms, you both need to be given a leaflet by your GP explaining the physical and emotional changes that the menopause brings, and what partners can expect to happen. GPs have leaflets on everything from bunions to teeth whitening, why not this?

Nick, 53 – There's nothing wrong with porn, if that's all there is on offer

I was first aware of the menopause when it happened to my mother. I didn't have a clue about what she was going through. More recently my wife has been going through it. I see it as a time when the ageing process is greatly accelerated, coupled with irrationality – certainly much more than before the menopause. There also seems to be a desire to pick fights for the sake of it. I find that really difficult. These fights are usually prompted by something the children want, and which I find totally unreasonable. Honestly, if you could hear us, you'd end up scratching your head, and wondering what the argument was really about.

Our sexual relationship has also gone out of the window. She gets these terrible night sweats. It's very uncomfortable for her, and she wakes up a lot. This has consequences for her mood. But she is clear that she would never go down the HRT route. She's always been committed to alternative medicine. We certainly can't have a rational conversation about that.

It wouldn't be fair or accurate to lay all the blame on the menopause. But I do think that it leads to some pretty prickly responses. The trouble is that when you're pissed off with your partner, you don't want to make love. I'm aware this also creates bad habits. If you believe you're going to be rejected, you stop asking, and then it becomes a habit not to. That then turns into the perceived norm.

I think it's unhealthy not to have sex regularly. Of course there are always ups and downs in a relationship, but it's difficult to end up angry with someone if you've had a jolly good bonk. That's the bottom line for most men. But, I wouldn't say I feel aggrieved about the lack of sex. It's more to do with mental and emotional frustration. Would I look elsewhere? That's an interesting question. I'm one of those blokes who believe it would be healthy to have a sophisticated brothel nearby run by an amusing, intelligent madam, where you can have good conversation and a drink, and if there was someone pretty knocking about who can provide a service without attachment so much the better. You could use the brothel in the same way as having a beer with your mates. It seems ridiculous that we don't bat an eyelid about having a massage just for sheer pleasure, which I do regularly at my club. Yet, if I was to ask for my old boy to be massaged, that would be the end of my membership. Then again, I certainly wouldn't tell my wife that I was going to a prostitute. But let me tell you, if I thought I could buy an insurance policy to make sure I didn't hurt anyone, and it prevented me picking up some disease, I would sign on the dotted line like a rat up a drain pipe.

How do I deal with the lack of sex? I call it DIY. Porn is readily available on the internet and I can't see anything wrong with it as long as it's legal. Okay, some porn sites are pretty disgusting, but I don't look at those. At the end of the day, a lot of sex – especially masturbatory sex – is about fantasy. That goes for women too. If a woman says she doesn't fantasize, she's a bloody liar. I have suggested watching porn with my wife. She expressed a kind of interest, but she didn't get into it. I'm not sure if she genuinely wasn't interested, or thinks she shouldn't be.

Mind you, I am not willing to have an affair. That's moving into the realms of dishonesty. In my book, having your togger pulled is quite a different matter from emotional involvement. That's when it gets destructive. You can understand why it happens though. Your wife starts to change, everything gets thrown out of sync, and in walks a sexy young thing. That's when the trouble starts. Our brains live in our balls. That overrides everything.

But I know this is not for me. I've heard too many stories of men of my age getting divorced and saying it's pretty grim being on the circuit again. Okay, some men do find it exciting. If they're wealthy, successful and don't look too much like Quasimodo, it's relatively easy to attract a younger woman. But I don't envy them for having to start all over again.

No, I'm very clear that I want to stay put in my marriage. Despite the arguments, and even though she drives me round the sodding bend – mind you, she would argue I do the same to her – I love her. She's the person I want to grow old with.

I think men do go through some kind of male menopause. But it's hard to recognize, because we don't have the same physical symptoms as women. It doesn't help living in a society which is still so hung up on sex either. My generation wasn't brought up to talk about it. I can remember my mother catching me masturbating when I was around 15. She gave me a huge lecture and said I was dirty and wrong in the eyes of God. She even said if she caught me again, she'd take me to a doctor. I can remember thinking what a ridiculous response, but when things like that have been drummed into your brain, it does have an effect. Yes, education and religion have had a very big impact on all of us who are now in our 50s and 60s. I think this is mirrored in how society portrays us. It makes me smile when I see people wearing pink ribbons for breast cancer. What about people wearing brown ribbons for prostate cancer. It just doesn't happen.

Will, 59 – Sex isn't just about penetration

I was married to a woman who went through the menopause just before we divorced. As our relationship wasn't brilliant, I accepted what was happening to her without questioning it. She was a scientist and dealt with it in a very matter of fact way: 'Get on with it, it will pass.' It didn't affect our sexual relationship because we didn't have one anyway.

I'm now in another relationship, and my new partner's also going through the menopause. It's a very different experience, mainly because she's been the love of my life since my early 20s. We went out for quite a long time when we first met, and I was devastated when she decided to end it. I carried this heartbreak all the way through the 31 years I was married to my first wife. It coloured everything.

After my wife and I divorced, I found her again through the internet. When we met, we didn't look at each other, we looked into each other. It's been like that ever since, and my grief is that I've had all those years without her.

It's not all plain sailing. Although I know what she's physically experiencing with the menopause, I find it very difficult to understand why she won't do anything about her weight. She's often moaning about it, but when I say 'get some exercise', she doesn't. It's not that the changes to her body have turned me off. Far from it – I look at the menopause as a natural phase in her cycle of life. But it does make me sad that she can't get motivated to help herself feel better about it. Yes, I suppose I am frustrated by her 'I can't be bothered' attitude. It's one thing for a woman to accept the menopause as inevitable, but another to let herself go.

Even so, it doesn't change the way I feel about her. It's who she is inside that really matters. My biggest struggle is not being able to pay her the sexual attention that she wants. Fading libido is not one of her problems. It's me who's experienced it. I suppose in a way

I've had the male equivalent of the menopause, not helped by some stressful issues I've had to deal with at work. I want at least to feel fired up enough to satisfy her. But I think a lot of men get stressed at my age and that affects their ability to have erections. I certainly know those 'Come on boy, let's get going' moments.

However, there's always more ways than one way to skin a cat. Personally, I've never been that fond of penetrative sex. If you know about anatomy, you'll understand that the vagina walls aren't sensitive. You're not going to give a woman a vaginal orgasm, because there's nothing there to do it. G-spot and clitoral orgasms are something else.

For me, sex is all about attention and care and I've always been the kind of man who wants to give pleasure more than receive it. Perhaps I've been influenced by what happened in my first marriage. I suppose you could have described it as a business arrangement more than anything else. My wife didn't enjoy sex for various reasons. I respected that. I didn't find it devastating to be rejected, just a bit disappointed and sexually frustrated. It certainly wasn't a big hassle when we parted, although she did say that she would be lonely for the rest of her life.

So it's been quite a readjustment to get used to the sexual needs of my present partner, especially when I feel so strongly for her. But I've come to realize that love-making depends on mood, situation and ambience. Sometimes it's lust, at other times caring, or passionate or it may be just a gentle sharing. Love and relationship are not just about sex. I think a lot of men are confused about that.

When we do make love, my partner often complains about vaginal dryness, but since I know how the female anatomy works I understand what's happening to her. We often use lubricants to help to stimulate her, but the most important thing is to forget your dick, and pay attention to what she needs. So lubricants don't bother me, although I think K-Y jelly is a bit bland.

I think it's dreadful how our society is affected by the commercialization of pornography being all about penetration. I think that gives a lot of men hang-ups about what sex should be. To some extent I also think women's sexual fantasies are misled by erotic writers like Jackie Collins. Everything focuses on 'that thrust.' It's a shame.

Personally, I've never talked about my sex life before to anyone, or about my partner being menopausal. I've never felt the need, but I hope this will help other men to realize sex isn't just about penetration. I also want to say that having a low libido isn't the end of the world either. I can go weeks without bothering about it, and quite honestly if I wasn't in a partnership I wouldn't bother with it at all. I look at a fading interest in sex as a natural progression to growing old.

But, if I was going to pass on advice to other men of my age, I would say it's time we got over the taboo of talking about sex. Those of us born in the 1950s were products of parents who had very Victorian attitudes. I got the impression that sex was about two things: procreation, and where posh people keep coal, and coal is dirty. You had to get on with it, but not enjoy it. If a girl got pregnant outside marriage it was the end of her. We're still dealing with elements of that. Those who were born at the end of the 60s and into the 70s didn't have parents with quite the same rigid attitudes, and I think this generation are much easier about the whole thing, and will probably experience menopause in a different way.

Gary, 67 – I suppose it was the male menopause

I was 54 when I had the affair, just when my wife was going through the menopause. The relationship was quite different from anything else I had experienced, and it was intensely painful to end it. Even so, deep down I knew I didn't want my marriage to be over. That's where I had made my commitment, and I realized pretty quickly how foolish it would be to set up home with a woman 20 years younger than me. It wasn't the right thing to do for any of us.

I often wonder whether I would have behaved like this if my wife and I had been able to talk about what she was going through. But when these things happen, it's never that simple. I suppose you could have described me as an accident waiting to happen. Apart from the menopause, the children were leaving home, we were moving house and I was moving jobs. Looking back I can see that I was more focused on the external changes happening around us than aware of how she might have been feeling. It caused a distance between us.

She didn't have mood swings or anything like that, but she did start to have pains in her joints which had never happened before. I don't know if she was in denial about what she was really experiencing, but it ended up with me shying away from speaking to her about anything to do with intimacy. I can remember finding this very difficult because I earned my living as a communications expert.

It just goes to show that what you teach is what you most need to learn.

Reflecting on what happened between the two of us, I can now see what a monumental change she went through. I always remember going together to see a doctor to talk through me having a vasectomy – we had four children, and I felt that was enough. During the interview, the doctor made the comment that he'd never come across another woman who valued motherhood so highly. My wife burst into tears because it made us both realize how much of her identify was wrapped up in being a mum, and – in a way – having a vasectomy meant that my function had been completed.

So, for me, everything intensified during her menopause. She moved from role of wife, mother and lover to this matriarchal authority figure. That was a real challenge for me. Being married to a postmenopausal woman makes you face your own ageing process. There's no escaping it. At the time I didn't understand any of this, so I reacted to what was happening by falling in love with a much younger woman. And, then of course, the damage is done.

I now realize I didn't want to face that I too was growing older. At the time, we were working in an environment with a lot of young people. It became very alluring and destructive because it made me question who I was, and inevitably I was drawn to the folly of youth. I ended up creating a bubble around myself so I could indulge my fantasy, dressing it up as a quest for the meaning of life. In fact I was thrashing around in the darkness, feeling very frightened and lost.

I never talked to friends about what was happening – I'm a very private person – but I did speak to a spiritual mentor I had at the time. He was more concerned over my welfare, and my wife's welfare, and what we could learn about ourselves than giving moral rectitude. I found that amazing. It helped me to see things differently, rather than punishing myself with yet more guilt.

For Western men, we don't have that deep understanding of life, or what happens to women's bodies as they go through these changes. As I see it, a woman is biologically led when she begins to menstruate. This is when she steps into her role of sexual being and ultimately, mother. When she reaches the menopause, it's spirituality-led. She steps away from what she was, to integrate truly with herself. It's like the phases of the moon. Everything she was is waning and everything she is to become is waxing. It's one of life's great paradoxes. It's the same for men, but in a completely different way. He sees his partner growing older and wants to hang onto being young, whether that's the fast car or the pretty young mistress. This is particularly prevalent in our Western society. There's so much pressure to claim youth. But, sadly, I think it's even more aggressive for women.

What advice would I give a man watching his wife go through the menopause? I think it's about developing an understanding of what an extraordinary time this is for a woman. It's about being prepared for the change that is going to happen. It's inevitable. In India, when a wife reaches the menopause, the husband will take himself off to ashrams to be with spiritual gurus, sometimes for years. He comes back after it's all blown over, and they get on with life in a new way. It's completely accepted within their culture.

So it's about being sympathetic and supportive, but at the same time being compassionate towards yourself, and what you're going through. Of course, we all react differently. A lot of men run away, like I did. But it's only kidding yourself.

I feel better having attempted to articulate what happened. It's the first time I have ever really reflected on what it was like. At the time you deal with what's happening in the moment. It's the only way you can get through these traumatic experiences.

I have still never sat down with my wife and really talked about it, which sounds odd after 43 years of marriage. I know I hold back because I don't want to hurt her, perhaps it was because my father walked out on my mother when I was eight. If my wife was to burst into tears I would feel awful. I would feel I have to fix it. That's my role as a man. That's what we're supposed to do.

These days we don't have sex at all. Of course I miss it. But I don't do anything about it. I try to enjoy my life for what it is right now. I would certainly never have another affair. It's been on offer a few times, but I always make it clear that I'm not available. Once you've gone through what I have, and put others through it too, you don't want to go there again. It involves a load of self-torture, recrimination, fire and brimstones. When you're young, you think about your genitals. The male menopause is about learning to say no to them.

Even though we don't have sex, my wife and I have forged a very strong bond. I've learned that love can come from this, rather than from sex in the biological sense. I think a lot of men get confused by that. What matters to me most is maturing, and being wise enough to carry on working on my relationship with my wife. Sure,

I could get upset about a lack of sex, but I've taken steps towards coming to terms with this, and embracing it rather than denying it. I feel desperately sorry for men who can't do that. Of course it's pleasurable to have loads of things, but it's worth remembering that they only last for a short time and they rarely bring meaningful joy. Yes, there are some things I regret, but life's like that. I don't hang on to them. I'll never be 50 again. I'll never have perfect teeth again. I'll never be able to do 101 things again. So?

John, 51 – It's not about sex, it's about pulling together

When I think of the menopause, I immediately think of my mother. I was 20 at the time. She didn't find it very easy. It certainly affected her psychologically as well as biologically. I did talk to her about it a bit, but it was such a taboo, and it still is. It certainly left me feeling confused.

I now regard the menopause as a natural progression to wisdom. I see that role for the older woman being just as important as producing the younger generation, but I do live in trepidation of my wife having it. She's not quite there yet. She's pretty robust, so I hope it will be a smooth transition. Having said that, one of her friends has had a very difficult time with her periods, and is so fed up that she keeps saying, 'Bring the menopause on.' But I don't think she knows what she's wishing on herself.

Speaking as a man who has entered his 50s, I believe we have a kind of menopause too. I am certainly much less of a sexual being these days. The urge doesn't have the insane drive that it used to when I was a younger man. It's a relief quite honestly. It means I can go out to parties and leave all that posturing behind. I can get on with being me, and actually enjoy it.

I married quite late – my children are still well under ten – and I was aware that sex was going to change after they came along. Actually, when I saw my children being born I knew what sex was all about. Before that I thought it was all about getting my leg over. Now I realize it's Mother Nature driving us to reproduce, and when that's been achieved, the need isn't so great any more. Well, it isn't for me anyway. That's not to say I live in a sexless marriage. We make love about twice a month. Yes, sometimes I do get frustrated, but that's okay too. I spent my whole life trying to gain some kind of control of my passionate side and like I say, sometimes it's a blessed relief not to be governed by it these days.

When I was 19, I could never have imagined saying this. I think a lot of young people imagine what sex will be like before they do it, and what it will feel like afterwards – all those endorphins being released. Sex isn't always like that at all. Sometimes it's a complete let-down. You pull your trousers up and get on with life feeling a bit shoddy. Being realistic about sex is what maturing teaches you, especially when you're in a long-term relationship. So, for me marriage is about forging a bond without using sex to get at each other or score points. It's really about the hard graft of learning how to juggle our jobs, raise our children and make the most of what we have.

Thinking about it, I realize I am much more inhibited about initiating sex than I used to be. It requires more delicacy. It's realizing and respecting what we want and need from each other – how we go about getting that. And, of course, we can spot the bullshit factor in each other straight away. I've never been one for asking her to dress up like a traffic warden, and she certainly doesn't want me strutting around like a storm trooper. Every time I've tried porn movies, it's left me feeling nauseous, and she has no interest in watching other people's sex acts. It's not about notches on the bedhead, especially when you're older parents. Although I am aware that some of my friends are still into that.

I think the way society talks about sex is ridiculous. It focuses on how many times you 'have it'. Sex isn't about having it. It's about relationship. Anyway, you can't measure what's okay for you against what's okay for someone else. There's always the danger of falling into that 'Well, he says he's getting it five times a week, what's wrong with my partner – because I'm not'. There's nothing about individual needs, or different times of life, or what happens during parenthood, or the menopause. It really is time to stop measuring sex like that, but I realize it's a complex matter.

I see older women as wise, fun and complex, with a lot of nous. That's one hell of a combination. But I would be lying if I said that given the choice of a woman who is postmenopausal, and a woman in her early 40s, of course I would be more attracted to the younger woman. You can't ignore the call of the evolutionary process, and the deep desire to procreate – and that means the woman having the lumps and bumps in the right place. Cruel, but true.

Sometimes I talk to friends – well, mainly one – which normally happens over a couple of pints. He has less sex than me, and he's very angry and frustrated about it. I can see how dangerous it's becoming to his marriage. I do talk to my wife occasionally. Recently I've been asking her what she needs from me, rather than thinking what she can do for me. That's helped. I also understand that she may be struggling with her body image, especially after having two children, and heading for the menopause. If you look at an image of Venus, she's always portrayed with a tidy neat figure, and doing something sensual with her hair. She's certainly not a mother figure, or a postmenopausal woman. We men get hooked on these images, and expect our wives to carry on looking the same until they're in their coffins. It's completely unrealistic, and I hate the way society dismisses the older woman.

The message is, 'You've done your bit, get lost', I've seen that happen all over the place: in supermarkets, on the road, in the workplace. Young women are often the worst. It's 'Move aside Granny, I'm a-coming through'. Except that Granny knows a hell of a lot about life, and certainly knows what's on the way. She could be of such help to the younger generation if only she was respected. In other cultures, such as Italy, it's still accepted for the grandmother to live with the family. She's the reminder to the rest of the family that one day age will come to them too. In our culture, we separate out from our old folk by putting them in nursing homes.

A woman's ageing process becomes a very touchy subject. The taboo is that the man marries the woman of his dreams. She is happy to have sex with him because this brings her security of some kind. Then she has children and Bingo! She doesn't want him in the same way any more. He starts to feel rejected, because up until now his whole conditioning has been about getting his leg over. She gets exasperated and bored, and starts wearing winceyette nightdresses. He starts withdrawing and asking 'Aren't I enough for you any more?' She shuts him out because she's too tired to deal with it. He goes off to have a hand-job, or starts looking at porn. Sometimes it's an affair with a younger woman. His wife finds out, and all hell breaks loose. This starts again when the woman hits the menopause and is no longer interested in sex.

It doesn't help that we no longer learn from each other any more. We spend all our time chasing material goods, watching mind-numbing programmes on television or reading in *Hello Magazine* about the size of Jordan's tits. There's no room to pass on real wisdom or guidance about, for example, how to manage difficult issues in relationships, or the changes that happen during the menopause.

As I see it, it's all about people's needs not matching any more. Not helped by the way the media, and society in general, promote self-interest: 'If only I had this', or 'if only I could do that'. It has turned into a toxic group activity which, to my mind, only just falls short of rape in warfare. The menopausal woman is caught right in the middle, until she moves beyond it and doesn't give a stuff any more.

Daniel, 66 – Different planets is an understatement

The most alarming thing was my partner's unpredictability. Life would be going well and then out of the blue, sometimes from one minute to the next, she'd turn into a crazy monster.

We'd been together for ten years, so I got used to her mood swings just before period time. I knew that things would calm down, and all would be well for another few weeks. But this was different. Sometimes it got so bad that I thought our marriage was over. In fact, I felt deceived, which made me very angry and resentful. I remember saying to her, 'I don't know who you are any more.'

It was a complete turn-off sexually. I didn't want to go near her. It was too dangerous because I never knew what kind of response I would get. I couldn't talk about it either, and it's taken a long time to learn to feel safe enough to do so. Luckily she's very open, and that's helped. But at the time, it was very difficult for me.

I now realize that I didn't handle it very well. I used to react and storm off, or go into massive sulks. In time, I began to understand that that didn't help. She's very sensitive to what happens in the world, especially the shitty parts of it. I can see now that her sensitivities were being heightened by the changes she was going through.

Why didn't I leave? Well, love isn't just about emotions; it's about a state of being. I've been married twice before, but when I met her, I just knew she was right for me. Knowing that helped me to work through what was going on for us. That's not to say I haven't sometimes imagined leaving. I chose to stay because she's an amazing person. I'm much more whole and human because of our relationship. Being involved in personal development and spiritual growth has also helped. It's given us the foundation to understand each other.

Our sex life has never been particularly easy. For one reason or another, it's always been quite painful for her, and this has caused us problems. For a man, it's hell to be fully aroused and then for your partner to stop you. It made me feel anger, rejection, rage, blame. The whole works really.

But this also means there wasn't a big change in our sex life when she became menopausal. It was more to do with the atmosphere. I can imagine if you're in a relationship that's always been great, sexually, it must be devastating for it to suddenly stop.

We don't even try to have penetrative sex any more. I would be lying if I said I don't miss it. Of course I do. It's a natural biological urge for a man. But we've arrived at a place where we enjoy sensuality more than sexuality. It's a whole-body experience, where we lie naked and entwined together and take pleasure in the touch of each other's skin. It's non-orgasmic, and we rarely involve genital sex, but it's taken me to a different level of relating and letting go. Funnily enough, I've discovered that when it does lead to orgasm, it spoils it. I never dreamed I would feel satisfied without penetration or orgasm. In fact, I never thought there was an alternative to penetrative sex. But I now realize there're lots of different ways to be sexual and sensual without involving genitals.

Men don't talk about this kind of thing in any intimate detail. It's normally a comment over a few pints with your mates about whether you got your end away. I certainly find it hard to talk about my sex life. Fine if it's good, but to admit that it isn't working makes me feel shame. I guess it's a social shame, because there seems to be this assumption that you have to have a great sex life until you're about in the grave. To admit you don't isn't the done thing. There's also an assumption that men know about sex, and how to have sex. But we don't, and we haven't got a clue when it comes to the menopause. I had no idea what to expect. My mother must have been through it, but I never knew anything at the time, apart from the odd joke about hot flushes and her forgetting things.

Actually, I realize I've never understood menstruation either. I have no idea what's going on in a woman's body. It's a total mystery. And, having been with a woman who has gone through the menopause, I now realize how dissimilar men and women are. Different planets is an understatement. I now grasp what a huge experience menstruation and the menopause must be, and, actually, how few women themselves understand it. If you think about it, a woman probably has over 400 periods in her life time. If you attended a seminar one week a month for 40-odd years, surely you would be highly experienced and knowledgeable about the subject matter. That's why I find it astonishing when women aren't prepared for what happens when they reach the menopause.

I don't think my partner knew what was happening to her either – not until she was almost over it. I was relying on her to tell me, so no wonder it was so chaotic. I began to realize something had changed when she kept on having hot flushes at night, and needed to move away from me. I thought she was rejecting me. If you don't know what's happening, it's obvious you're going to think that.

My partner is still as feminine as she was before the menopause. So the changes aren't about physical appearance so much as learning more about life. It's certainly helped that both of us are open to exploring sensuality. I think you need help, even if it's a book that you can read together.

I know I would have been pushed to the limit if we hadn't found a way to express intimacy. I am pretty sure I would have sought out sex elsewhere. I do masturbate fairly regularly though. I would never do it with her. I think that's because I still have a hang-up over public school stuff about guilt and shame. It's taken me a while to accept it's my body. It's a nice experience and there's nothing wrong with it. I suppose it's like getting hungry. You have a desire to eat, so you have a meal. It's as simple as that. But I'm not into porn or prostitutes. That wouldn't work for me.

It's been good to talk openly about this. Enlightening even. It's made me more aware of how the media speak about sex. It's so misrepresentative. I also don't like the way sex has become so medicalized either. I wouldn't take Viagra. I don't have problems with erection, and even if I did, I've reached the realization that I've had some great sex in my life, and *so what* if I don't again. It wouldn't stop the depth of intimacy that my partner and I now enjoy.

Okay, I'm going to come clean. Without exception, by the time the interviews came to an end I had fallen in love with each one of these men. I was truly taken aback by their wisdom and willingness to talk to me so openly and honestly about such very intimate things. They can join my girls' club anytime.

I think these interviews prove how important it is to give men a chance to speak up. They care about what's happening to us, but they don't necessarily have the same communication skills as we do. Even more important, men need the information to help them understand what is really going on when they feel pushed out by our irritability, hot flushes and vaginal atrophy.

In that spirit, I hope that our last 'M' word chapter, managing the menopause, may be of as much practical help to men as I trust it will be for women.

CHAPTER 6

Managing the menopause

This final M-word chapter looks at practical ways to manage the menopausal transition, from how to get the best out of your GP and coming off HRT, to exploring alternative medicine and keeping fit in mind and body. But let's start with women's experiences of talking to doctors, especially when it comes to sex.

Talking to doctors

Although I had been disappointed and frustrated by my own visit to my GP when I began to find sex painful, I was astonished how angry some of the women I interviewed were about many doctors' inability to talk comfortably and confidently about sex. 'Why *is* it so difficult for doctors?' asked one woman. 'It makes me feel bloody angry, and helpless.'

Fifty-eight-year-old Katherine had attempted to find information about different vaginal creams to help dryness, but had experienced her doctor as embarrassed and dismissive. Katherine found little support at the pharmacy either. 'If your doctor can't give you advice, and pharmacies don't know, where *do* you go?' she said. 'I've been with my GP for 19 years,' said another woman, who is gay. 'She was very good about the practicalities of the menopause, but she never once mentioned sex.'

Some interviewees on medication following breast cancer treatment said they were very ill-informed about how the drugs could affect their sex life. 'What information did I have about my sex drive being affected when I was put on Amiridex?' said Beryl, clearly still very distressed. 'The answer is NOTHING. Whenever I've asked, everyone just turned away and blushed.' She added with some bitterness, 'You go through cancer, and you're bloody happy to be alive, but when you want to find out about trivial things like sex, who is there to turn to?'

Another woman in her mid-50s said that in her experience, GPs don't understand how emotionally difficult it is when you realize everything has changed.

> I got very upset the other day. I had sex with my husband and realized it was sore. In fact, I felt I had been grazed. I went to my GP to see what I could get to help. As I was lying on the couch having an internal examination, a thought hit me. I realized I was beginning another stage of life and I now had to ask for help in order to have sex. It was awful.
>
> I was given a prescription for Vagifem pessaries, and walking into town to the chemist, I suddenly felt old, as if I was on the scrapheap. Done the kids. Now it was about looking after ageing parents. I was also so embarrassed about having to see the doctor about sex that I hid the pessaries from my husband. I've come to terms with it a bit more now, but I have no idea where to find someone sensible to talk to about it.

Sensible resources

Seeking someone sensible, I turned to Renée, the manager of the UK's first all-women's sex shop, intriguingly called Sh!. Renée has been with the company since its early days and has a refreshingly down-to-earth attitude about the sexual and emotional difficulties of the menopause. She told me that many of her older female customers come to the shop precisely because they can't talk to their doctor. 'One woman came in some distress following a visit to her GP,' she told me. 'She'd been given lubricant with an applicator to help her vaginal dryness. She got the impression she wasn't meant to touch herself, and actually thought there was something wrong with her because of it.'

Renée continued,

> We had a good chat about it, and I advised her to throw the applicator away and apply the lubricant herself. I explained how she could play with it, use her fingers, or a sex toy, or get her partner to do it. Lubricants can be very sexy. She was amazed!

Renée is concerned about how most doctors talk about sex in purely clinical terms, especially when it involves older women going through the menopause.

Sometimes we have medical groups who come here, and they have
no idea what we do. In fact, they are often shocked when we tell
them about lubricants and sex toys, and how we encourage women
to explore their bodies. But there must be a need for this kind of
education, otherwise our shop would not be as successful as it is.

Renée and her team are happy to talk about any aspect of sex, no
matter how old a woman is. Sometimes they have to explain even
the most basic facts about how female genitals work.

We have a little soft vulva we call Rosie, which we use to point out
areas that feel good. This opens up discussion about all sorts of things
the woman has never spoken about before. So this is the place where
they can come when they feel a bit down, have a cuppa and a chat,
buy a sex toy if they want to, or just go away feeling more confident
about themselves. It's too easy for women who have had busy family
lives to forget the sexy side of themselves. They may have got used
to dull sex on a Saturday night, more because their husband wants it,
and have forgotten how to get turned on. This is far more common
than you would imagine.

Even though it didn't do much to raise my own libido – I fear this
might be a lost cause – I would highly recommend a visit to Sh!. I
spent a thoroughly enlightening and enjoyable afternoon there, and
even came away with a delicious-smelling candle that when lit, turns
into erotic massage oil. Ok, it's still waiting unused beside our bed,
but at least it's there for when the moment might be right. Who
knows . . . In the meantime, you can find contact details for Sh! at
the end of the book.

Another excellent resource is Simply Hormones, a website created
by Kathryn Colas who we met in Chapter 2. She set it up when she
herself reached the change of life, and realized there was virtually no
information relevant to the lifestyle of modern menopausal women.
As far as she was concerned, most of us disappear off the public radar
unless we have gynaecological problems or other medical conditions.
'Usually a visit to your doctor results in a prescription for some kind
of life-numbing drug,' she said, 'and then you're sent home.'

You can't fix the menopause. But knowing about it can help. In
my own case, I went through ten years of hell. I suffered from low
self-esteem and got to the point where I didn't know what I was

on the planet for. I also began to suffer from vaginal atrophy and couldn't understand what was wrong with me. I started to reject my husband, which caused a lot of rows. It was only when I went to a conference and heard someone speak about it that I realized what was happening to me.

As we have heard from the women at the beginning of the chapter, Kathryn is not the only one who has felt frustrated with the lack of medical information and support. So I decided to talk to a GP myself to find out the best way of approaching menopausal issues.

Getting the best from your GP

In the UK, GPs are usually the first port of call for women experiencing menopausal symptoms, although some patients may already have a gynaecologist who will provide treatment. I was surprised to learn that there are specialist menopausal clinics located throughout the UK. However, most women who go seem to be referred by GPs when they are suffering from other physical or mental health issues in addition to menopausal ones.

When I tackled Adrian, a thoroughly delightful and enlightened GP from the West Country, about the experiences of my interviewees, he agreed that when it comes to the menopause, some doctors might not be as empathetic as they could be. He also pointed out that GPs aren't there to provide counselling, although, of course, they should certainly listen carefully to what the patient is telling them. However, a GP's main job is to identify symptoms, prescribe treatment and refer on to a specialist if needed. Adrian also reminded me of the pressure GPs work under.

We have ten minutes allotted for each patient to make these very important assessments. So, I don't think it's fair to say that GPs don't listen or take menopausal women seriously any more than someone, for instance, who has osteoporosis.

Adrian's primary concern is to check whether a woman presenting with menopausal symptoms has other underlying health issues. 'I can tell you,' he said, 'whatever symptoms a woman may be anxious about, her GP will often also be worried about something else.'

Nevertheless, Adrian also believed it was down to the woman to tell the GP what was worrying her, rather than leaving it to the doctor to second-guess or let things slide by. 'If her doctor doesn't ask what is going on emotionally, there can be misunderstandings and frustration, particularly if the woman is feeling sensitive anyway.'

Adrian also pointed out that many women blame the menopause for other things going wrong in their life, and expect the GP to fix it.

> A good GP *will* recognize that a woman going through the menopause may well be undergoing other major life changes. Children leaving home. Parents dying. Perhaps a failing marriage. All these events have to be taken into account to give the right kind of support. It can be a very sensitive time in her life.
>
> But, for some women, it can be too easy to look at the menopause as a skip into which you can tip all the rubbish that life has thrown at you over the past couple of decades. Life is a far more complicated biological–psychosocial mix than that.

After speaking to Adrian, I understood much better what is appropriate to expect from GPs. From the interviewees we heard from at the beginning of the chapter, it's clear there needs to be more recognition and validation from our doctors about the way the menopause affects us. At the same time, it's up to us to take responsibility and make sure we get the best out of any meeting we do have with our GPs. So, I have summarized the points that Adrian made:

- *The GP is not a counsellor.* He/she is there to assess your overall state of health, and to act as a signpost to other specialists if there are underlying concerns. (By the way, I've found it doesn't necessarily follow that female doctors are any more sympathetic to menopausal women than male ones are.)
- Be clear about what you want to talk to your GP about. His or her time is limited, but you will be offered follow-up appointments if necessary. Writing a list of things you want to talk about before your appointment can help.
- The GP may offer a variety of tests, for example, to assess thyroid function. If you don't understand what these tests are, or why they are needed, make sure you ask for information. You may also be referred on to gynaecologists or menopause clinics.
- Don't forget that the menopause is a time of immense physical, mental and emotional change. You may be grieving all kinds of losses, and finding it hard to make sense of things. Your GP

may not in fact be the best person to talk to on this. Instead, this could be a good time to see a counsellor.

- Finally, the way you experience the menopause is very personal to you. So do take the time to inform and educate yourself about the changes you're going through, especially when it comes to HRT.

The HRT conundrum

I have already said that I chose to go through the menopause naturally. But, I was fortunate not to suffer from debilitating symptoms. Others are not so lucky. Hormone replacement therapy or HRT has certainly been very helpful in delaying the menopause for younger women who have had hysterectomies or cancer treatments. It has also helped those with early onset arthritis and osteoporosis. So I don't intend to stand in moral judgement about whether it's right or wrong to take it. That has to be down to advice from doctors and your personal choice.

However, many women I spoke to who had taken HRT were completely unprepared for what happened when they came off it, especially when they did so abruptly. They specifically asked me to include their experiences, to warn other women who may have no idea of what they will go through.

Basic facts about HRT

Before hearing from women about their experiences of HRT, here's some basic information. HRT is mostly made with synthetic or non-human hormones, designed to replace the body's oestrogen that falls naturally during the menopause. HRT works by artificially *delaying* the menopause, and therefore helps to relieve symptoms such as hot flushes, mood swings and painful sex. It does not prevent or stop the menopause. At whatever age a woman ceases taking HRT, menopausal symptoms will usually return to some degree.

Most HRT taken today is produced by three methods: 1. So-called conjugated oestrogen, made from the urine of pregnant horses, collected, I understand, by catheter. (The mares declined to comment, and apparently the urine of pregnant camels is now also being used.) 2. Esterified oestrogens, made from plant compounds. 3. Synthetic oestrogens, artificially produced in the laboratory.

HRT comes in different combinations and dosages, and is

prescribed as patches, implants, gels, creams and pills. Some women have no problems taking it, but research suggests that others may be at some enhanced risk of breast cancer or heart disease. This means that, generally, GPs are increasingly reluctant for women to use HRT for longer periods of time. When you come off HRT, discuss with your doctor how to do this best, to minimize the effects of hormonal withdrawal.

There are new hormone replacement treatments coming onto the market all the time, for example bioidentical hormone replacement therapy (BHRT). This is a supplement of steroid hormones identical to those produced in the body, and is used to slow down the ageing process. Again, using these products has to be a personal choice.

Localized HRT is a different product. It has very low synthetic hormone levels, which help to plump-up the vagina to make sex more comfortable, but without significantly affecting the rest of the body. It is inserted into the vagina as pessaries, creams or a ring.

HRT and sex: a short recap

Some of my interviewees wanted to know how HRT evolved into the treatment of choice for women with low libidos. I won't go into detail about the HRT story – Louise Foxcroft covers this brilliantly in *Hot Flushes, Cold Science*. Other good sources are Gail Sheehy's *The Silent Passage* and Judith Houck's *Hot and Bothered: Women, Medicine and the Menopause*. But here are some salient points.

Although HRT was first prescribed in the 1950s to ease menopausal symptoms, it shot into the limelight in the late 60s following the publication of Robert Wilson's controversial book, *Feminine Forever*. Wilson, a British-born gynaecologist who practised in New York, described the menopause as 'a serious, painful and often crippling disease', but one that HRT could miraculously cure: 'No longer need she fret about the cruel irony of women ageing faster than men.' Wilson also promoted HRT as the cure-all for low or non-existent libidos. 'It is simply no longer true that the sexuality of a woman past 40 necessarily declines more rapidly than that of her husband.'

The book became an instant bestseller and persuaded doctors and menopausal women alike that HRT was not just 'helpful, but essential'. As a consequence, millions of women around the world were prescribed it.

Things changed after 2002 when a Women's Health Initiative

study suggested that long-term use of some types of HRT increased the risk of breast cancer and heart disease. Millions of women stopped taking it, and immediately experienced a return of menopausal symptoms, including loss of libido. Those who chose to stay on it had to live with the anxiety that – far from being the promised miracle cure – HRT did have possibly significant side effects.

Since the 2002 study, safer forms of HRT have been developed to relieve uncomfortable symptoms, and also to help with sex drive. Today, the Women's Health Initiative suggests that short-term HRT (three years) is low-risk for women under 60, particularly those who do not have a family history of breast or ovarian cancer or heart disease.

'There's no doubt that women on HRT are much more sexually active,' Professor Lorraine Dennerstein told me. 'However, it's important to take health risks into consideration.'

I asked her what was available for women who don't want to take HRT. 'There are new sex treatments being developed that act on neurotransmitters in the brain,' she said. She had no qualms about this new 'Viagra for women'. 'Why should women be deprived of sexual desire, when it is distressing for them?'

I understand her point, but am disturbed by how much information on the menopause still seems to push sex 'treatments' as general menopausal cure-alls. Several alternative health professionals I interviewed were also concerned. One said,

> There is so much media pressure to stay looking young for as long as possible. Women are still led to believe HRT will put off their ageing process. But that's not true. It may plump up your skin and slow down muscular diseases such as osteoporosis and arthritis, but as soon as you come off it – which you will have to do at some point – you go through the menopause anyway.

Another said,

> Menopause is not a life-threatening issue. It's a natural part of a woman's life cycle. However, some women think HRT will resolve everything that might be going wrong. That's not true. The menopause tends to bring everything that is unresolved to the surface which needs to be looked at. When you stop taking HRT, whatever this is will still come up then. But women aren't prepared for this.

Alexandra Pope, who educates women about menstruation, is concerned that women often go from taking the contraceptive pill straight onto HRT. This means a woman's whole sexual history has been controlled by other hormones than those of her own body.

> These women have never had a chance to feel their own natural body rhythms. Yes, they may be tremendously successful, fearsome even – think of Maggie Thatcher who made it known that she used HRT to legitimize her power in the eyes of her male colleagues – but I wonder how many women sit down and wonder about who they *really* are.
>
> A woman's natural menstrual cycle keeps her connected to herself and to her body. She can notice monthly changes and learn how she can support herself during her cycle. The changes that happen during the menopause take her much deeper into herself, and challenge her to accept herself in a new way.
>
> So, I would say that there is something soulless about women who allow themselves to be controlled by these replacement hormone treatments.

Hananja Brice-Ytsma, a herbalist and senior tutor at the Archway Clinic of Herbal Medicine in London, is also concerned about how HRT can interfere with the body's natural rhythms.

> We all age naturally. The body is geared to finding the best ways of functioning during this process; how it can maintain harmony with itself. This is the way of staying truly healthy. When you start interfering with this, it can impede the body's system from creating a natural balance.

Women talking about HRT

Many women I interviewed share Alexandra's and Hananja's concerns. One woman, who has used only alternative therapies to help her through the menopause, said she would never consider taking anything that would cover up 'the profound experience that the menopause brings'. However, she acknowledged she was lucky with her menopause, and knew of other women who go through hell. She added, 'I realize they may need something more to help them than just herbal remedies.'

Another interviewee worried about cancer, but her main objection to HRT was realizing that as soon as she stopped taking it, she would go through the menopause anyway. 'The menopause is about getting older. I accept that. Why not go through the change when my body is telling me it's the right time?'

Josie is a 62-year-old artist's model, which means she poses naked for students of all ages. She was put off HRT after her neighbour took it.

> She's ten years older than me. She went on HRT because she wanted to stay younger. But she had to come off it eventually, which meant all her symptoms had just got delayed. So I didn't think it was worth it. It only puts off the sagging and bagging for a while, and the art students aren't bothered by what I look like. They just want a model to draw.

However, when Katrina, a board director of a high-profile public relations company, went through the menopause, she felt pressurized to take HRT. It had a profound effect on the way she thought about herself.

> I took HRT because it was the fashion. I didn't want to think that I was ageing. I didn't want those lines on my face, or to lose my looks. However, after about two years I came off it because I felt I was compromising who I was. I didn't like that at all.
>
> When I came off HRT, I also took the decision not to have Botox. This was difficult. Most women I know in my working life do a lot of Botox. I had to tell myself that I didn't *have* to go with the flow. I was okay with who I was without it. It can make you feel very lonely though. I'm sure it's not the same in rural areas, but in a glamorous, hard-living city like London, it's a big thing not to do it.

Another woman felt pressured by her doctor into taking HRT. She had just discovered her husband had been having an affair.

> The doctor I saw seemed very keen for me to take it. She told me I needed to understand that the world had no place for older women. When she said that, I felt the bottom had dropped out of my world. I was only in my mid-40s and my eldest child was just 16. It felt like this doctor had given me a death sentence. I ended up in floods of tears.
>
> I went back again to get the results of the menopause test, which,

of course, was positive. She made out my prescription for HRT and said women were never meant to have the menopause. In the old days we would have died. It was only afterwards that I realized the doctor, who was well into her 60s, was probably taking HRT herself, which is why she was so defensive about it.

For others, taking HRT has raised some existential issues. Even though Barbara regards HRT as a lifesaver for halting her arthritis and enabling her to continue a very good sex life with her husband, she often thinks it is 'weird' to have arrived at the age of 65 without having gone through the menopause. She told me, 'It's as if I've bypassed something very important, which I can't quite put my finger on.'

Another woman, also in her late 60s, told me that although HRT had made it possible for her to remain sexually and physically active, she was beginning to grow concerned.

I'm frightened about how I am going to die. I've been on HRT for almost 30 years. I am terrified that if I stop it, my body will age overnight. But if I go on taking it, will I just keep going for ever? I mean, how *will* I get old?

I was at a loss to know how to respond to her, and it left me feeling rather glad that I have decided to age the way nature intended.

Coming off HRT

I've read too many informational leaflets that suggest there are few, if any, side effects when coming off HRT. The experience of many women I spoke to tells a different story. One described the information from her GP as 'appalling'. 'Doctors should highlight the fact that when you stop HRT you will go straight into menopause, especially if you come off it quickly.'

Another woman was taken off HRT after her new doctor expressed concern about the length of time she had been on it. 'When it was first prescribed, I was led to believe that HRT would bypass the menopause. This wasn't true. The only thing it did bypass was my periods. I've all the rest of the symptoms and those wretched hot flushes are still going on.'

Several women spoke about being prescribed HRT after a hysterectomy, but said they had been given no information about what would happen when they stopped taking it. Natalie, now 62, had a particularly rough time.

> My gynaecologist suggested a total hysterectomy because I had fibroids, which meant I was bleeding heavily most of the time. After surgery, he put me straight onto HRT. 'This is easy,' I thought. 'Menopause by appointment. I don't understand what menopausal women are moaning on about.'
>
> I honestly thought that by taking HRT I would avoid the menopause. And this is a highly qualified nurse speaking here.
>
> When I reached 60, my GP suggested it was time I stopped taking HRT. That's when the trouble kicked in. Even though I did it gradually, it was horrendous. I couldn't sleep, my joints ached and I felt depressed, temperamental, sad, unstable and vulnerable. I also suddenly felt old, especially as I began to lose my hair.
>
> It was very hard on my partner. I would weep at the slightest thing that happened between us, and nothing she could do was right. These feelings were so all-consuming that I felt they came from the core of my being. In fact, I would even describe them as primal.

Natalie became so distressed that she went back to her GP and demanded to be put back onto HRT right away. Instead, the GP persuaded her to go through the transition using natural remedies. Gradually, she says, her symptoms subsided, and life got back on an even keel.

> I'm glad now that I didn't go back onto HRT. It's allowed something deeper to come through which has helped me to acknowledge I am at a different stage in life. It's also helped me to take back control of my body. I've now got my weight in check, and because my hair never recovered, I also wear a wig. That's made a huge difference to my confidence.

After taking HRT for several years following a hysterectomy, Charlotte also had a very difficult time when she came off it.

> A hysterectomy followed by HRT gives you a false menopause. You get it full on when you come off it. I found it very difficult. Hot flushes, mood swings, lack of sexual desire, all that stuff. It's your body reacting to the lack of hormones, even if they are artificial. You can't escape it.

I also suffered from some pretty dramatic mood swings, which forced to me to look at what really mattered. That's when my relationship broke up. You get to see what's really there after the sex goes out of it.

Charlotte spoke for several interviewees about the way HRT tends to mask existing emotional problems. Just as physical symptoms return, unresolved emotional issues also tend to resurface once you stop taking HRT. If you start feeling distressed once you stop HRT, as I have suggested throughout the book, do seek help.

Localized HRT

A number of interviewees said that although they hadn't considered using full-on HRT, they found localized HRT, such as Vagifem (another ghastly name), helped greatly with vaginal dryness and painful sex. Sixty-three-year-old Frances uses it regularly.

As soon as I stopped HRT, sex became really painful. It put me right off. So I started using localized HRT pessaries. My gynaecologist said 'You have to look at it like this. You've got a lovely skin because you moisturize it. You have to do the same for your vagina. You can only do that with these pessaries.'

It worked. Sex is much more pleasurable, but the pessaries do have side effects, one of them being weight gain. I'm a professional dancer and teacher, and that's been hard for me.

Gail, who is in her mid-50s, had also found localized HRT helpful.

We still occasionally have penetrative sex, although not as much as we used to. It definitely makes the vagina more supple, and stops all that dryness and discomfort. I would certainly recommend it to women who were having similar problems.

Lucy, also in her 50s, agrees.

I was prescribed localized HRT when I couldn't have a vaginal swab. Sometimes it was so painful it made me scream, and I also bled afterwards. Localized HRT has made a huge difference, and to my sex life with my husband as well. Yes, I know it's HRT, but in minute amounts. It's not going into my system. I would certainly encourage women to use it. Mind you, I wouldn't bother with it if it wasn't for my husband.

Aha! I thought. Yet another menopausal woman who, if she's honest, admits to having sex far more for her husband's sake than her own. Seems to be a continuing theme.

Things to be aware of if you want to take HRT

HRT unquestionably helps some women with medical conditions, and can generally help to prolong your sex life. But HRT can't stop the ageing process, and, once you come off it, no matter what age, you will probably develop menopausal symptoms.

If you decide that HRT is for you, do some research so you can know about the pros and cons. Make sure you ask your GP about all the risk factors. While taking it, you should be given regular checks at your GP's surgery, including blood pressure and breast screening.

Let's now look at how alternative medicine can help.

Natural alternatives

More and more women, I found, are looking for ways to manage the menopause naturally. Most of my interviewees who had either come off HRT or had never taken it were using alternative methods to reduce symptoms and boost their general health and well-being. Many were using herbal remedies with considerable success, so I jumped at the chance of going to a seminar for practising herbalists. Led by Hananja Brice-Ytsma, the seminar was wonderfully titled *Flushed, Fat and Fifty: The Menopause Doesn't Have to be Like This*. As well as researching the book, I wanted to see if there was anything that could help me more personally

During the day, many herbalists gave positive accounts of how herbs can help to relieve symptoms such as hot flushes, but not much seemed to help flagging libidos. One practitioner said that in her experience – same old story – most women don't talk about the lack of sexual desire unless specifically asked. 'I think it's just too embarrassing,' she said. Someone else quipped, 'The brain is the main sexual organ, anyway. It's all about telling yourself you want it.'

I agree that, under normal circumstances, sex can be a mental choice. But since the neural transmitters to the brain are affected when oestrogen levels fall, telling a menopausal woman that she can choose to have sex simply doesn't help. Perhaps only women suffering from a low-to-non-existent sex drive or painful sex can understand how exasperating and dismissive it is to hear a comment like this. I noticed that the herbalist who made the remark had some way to go before reaching menopausal age herself. But it did make me think, that even in a seminar with enlightened health professionals such as these, low libido and painful sex tends to be treated as a bit of a joke.

After the workshop, I asked Hananja if vaginal atrophy is a lifelong condition. 'For some women it can be,' she said. 'It depends on overall health.'

> Dryness isn't just about the vagina. It can affect the eyes and mucus in the nose. If you have good circulation and look after your diet and take plenty of exercise, your mucus membranes are more likely to stay healthy. Sometimes, women presenting with this problem can have an underlying health issue, so it's always important to see your doctor to make sure there's nothing else going on that needs attention.

Personally, I eat well and am pretty healthy. I have no problems with mucus in my eyes or nose, although I have noticed my hair getting drier. So for me, VA is less about suspect processes in my body and more about the natural responses to an entirely normal lack of oestrogen.

But, talking with Hananja, I wasn't just interested in sex. I also wanted to know about something else that was causing me, in all honesty, more concern than losing my libido. 'Why,' I asked her, 'am I constantly finding myself upstairs forgetting what I am doing there, or finding myself staring blankly at an open fridge when I am already holding the milk bottle in my hand.'

'Ah!' she said knowingly. 'That's also down to diminishing oestrogen, which directly affects the way neurotransmitters respond in the brain.'

> We're not so bright any more, it's as simple as that. Women do get worried that they may be getting Alzheimer's. It's not that exactly, but there is a physiological reason why we become increasingly forgetful. It's part of the natural ageing process.

I was reassured to know it's normal as we get older to struggle to remember names and details. Maybe the way to get round this is to make lists – and then of course, try not to forget where you've put them.

I also felt compelled to ask Hananja about my weight changes. This, for me, has been one of the most distressing factors of the menopause. No matter how often I go to the gym, that roll of fat around my stomach won't go away. Other women experienced the same. One interviewee lamented that she could eat nothing but lettuce leaves, and would still put on weight. I know the feeling.

'Falling oestrogen levels again, I'm afraid,' said Hananja.

Your metabolism slows down as the levels of oestrogen diminish in the ovaries. The body needs oestrogen to help it adjust to the changes that happen at menopause, so it will look for oestrogen in other parts of the body, for instance in fat cells. Collecting these fat cells causes a redistribution of weight around the stomach and hips. This is perfectly normal, and this weight shift acts as protection for the organs and bones. Skinny people have less oestrogen to draw on, which is why they can have more severe menopausal symptoms.

I felt slightly reassured, but I continue to look dolefully at size 12 dresses hanging on shop rails.

My last question to Hananja was about the usefulness of natural progesterone cream, because I hadn't found it very helpful, certainly when it came to boosting my sex drive. These creams are not licensed in this country, so can only be obtained on the internet. Hananja had her doubts. She told me that when you reach the menopause, you no longer have progesterone, so you don't actually need it. 'It's oestrogen that's the problem. So why give your body something it no longer requires?'

Nevertheless, other women swore by it. One woman I spoke to described natural progesterone as a 'lifesaver'. 'I had terrible premenstrual tension,' she told me, 'and then hot sweats when the menopause arrived. I don't suffer from any symptoms now, and I know it's down to using my progesterone cream.' I asked her if it had helped with her libido. 'I don't know,' she said. 'I haven't had sex with my husband for ages.'

If you want to find out more about natural progesterone, John Lee's book *What Your Doctor May Not Tell You About Menopause: The Breakthrough Book on Natural Progesterone*, comes highly recommended by some interviewees.

Herbal remedies

For information on where to find qualified herbal practitioners, go to www.nimh.org.uk

Create a healthy gut

Food and natural medicines, including herbal remedies, need a healthy gut to be absorbed into the body. Constipation and diarrhoea indicate an unhealthy gut.

What can help

- Green vegetables
- Linseed (flaxseed)
- Miso (fermented soya)
- Nuts
- Rye bread (appears to lower risk of breast, colon and prostate cancer)
- Seaweed foods
- Soya
- Tofu
- Whole grains
- Cider vinegar, one capful in hot water, twice a day

Change in hormone levels

Indicated by bloating, breast swelling, tenderness, mood swings and headaches

What can help

- Slippery elm
- Drinking lots of water
- Green tea (as opposed to black)

To lessen hot flushes

- Black cohosh
- Red clover
- Dong quai

To lift and stabilize mood

- Black cohosh
- St John's wort

Vaginal atrophy/painful sex/dryness
What may help
- Asparagus racemosis (not the type you eat) helps to increase mucus in vagina
- Calendula pessaries, inserted every night, can help vaginal dryness
- Hops
- Marigold pessaries
- Aloe vera together with vitamin E oil
- Vitamin E oil on its own
- Black cohosh

What doesn't help
- Coffee (interferes with oestrogen levels and can raise anxiety levels)
- Cakes, white bread, sugar (raise adrenaline levels and can therefore increases feelings of anxiety)
- Alcohol
- Stress

Natural lubricants

A number of women I spoke to asked for a list of natural lubricants, because they didn't know where to look for them.

There are many lubricants on the market, but here's a selection that interviewees have either spoken about or recommended, most of which fall into the 'natural' category. They can be bought over the counter, or through the internet:
- **Astroglide** (water-based. Blurb claims to 'kick the menopause out')
- **K-Y jelly** (generally got the thumbs down)
- **Lubrin** (vaginal inserts made from natural products)
- **Replens** (apparently lasts up to three days after sex)
- **Sh! liquid** (water-based)
- **Sylk** (contains kiwi fruit extract)
- **The Durex range** (a truly bewildering array of products)
- **Yes** (water-based).

You may need to try a few before you find the right one.

Dealing with hot flushes

Many of the women I interviewed talked about the distress of having hot flushes. A hot flush can last from a few seconds to up to 15 minutes, but rarely more than an hour. Research suggests that up to three-quarters of women going through the menopause will experience hot flushes to some degree. Eighty-five per cent will continue to have hot flushes for more than one year, and 50 per cent for five years. Some women I interviewed were still having them ten years later, while others had taken HRT to stop them.

Hot flushes can be triggered by eating spicy or acidic foods (pickles, citrus, tomatoes), some red meats, white sugar and saturated fats such as margarine. Smoking tobacco can do the same, as can taking caffeine (coffee, black tea, cola, chocolate), alcohol or using recreational drugs such as marijuana. Hot weather, saunas and intense exercise can do it as well.

Hot flushes are by themselves physically uncomfortable, but they can also be aggravated by emotional stress, especially pent-up rage or grief. This can cause general anxiety, and if severe, panic attacks and heart palpitations.

So, what can you do yourself to manage them? Psychologists have developed a pilot study to train women in CBT (cognitive behavioural therapy) techniques to help them recognize what triggers a hot flush, and to reduce their levels of distress. This has been so successful that further studies are being considered. But to be honest, it isn't rocket science.

Several interviewees told me how they had instinctively developed their own coping strategies. For instance, one woman learnt to recognize that she always got a hot flush when she started to worry about money. This had prompted her to take better control of her finances. Another woman decided to change her perception that hot flushes were 'bad' experiences. Instead, she trained herself to wait patiently for them to pass. 'Knowing they don't last that long takes the stress out of it,' she said.

Another woman was encouraged by a friend to regard each hot flush as a spiritual cleansing process. 'My friend told me to imagine, every time they happened, that I was taking part in a Native American Indian sweat-lodge purification ceremony. Surprisingly, it helped.'

There are lots of creative ways to reduce the anxiety of hot flushes, and you can have great fun thinking up ways to deal with them. The important thing to know is they are a symptom that shows your body is changing, and one day they *will* stop. It may also help to know that although it can feel embarrassing to be constantly ripping your cardigan on and off, people you're talking to rarely notice that anything unusual is happening for you – unless, of course, you choose to say so. Which can in itself also help.

Several women I interviewed found night sweats far more difficult to cope with. Some got so hot they couldn't bear their partners to cuddle up to them, and sometimes their sweats were so severe that they had to change the sheets.

Sleeping separately

Needless to say, the casting off of bedding and the flinging open wide of windows, even in the depth of winter, can have interesting impacts on your relationship with the person who's sharing your bed. So can a general change of sleeping habits that often happens with the menopause.

Personally, I rarely sleep through the whole night these days even though I don't have night sweats. My pattern is to have a couple of good nights followed by several bad ones. I have come to accept this is going to happen so it doesn't cause me distress any more. However, I'm aware that a grunt or snore from my husband just when I'm dropping off has the potential to turn me into a maniacal killer. So we had a good chat about it, and changed our sleeping arrangements to suit us both. We go to bed together, but I will slip out to the spare room after my husband has fallen asleep. This means I can read my book well into the night or, indeed, listen to the World Service on Radio 4. (I often wonder how many menopausal women contribute to its listener figures.) Early morning, one of us gets up to make the tea, and we climb back into bed together to enjoy a shared start to our day. For us, this works well.

Many women, I found, would also prefer to sleep separately from their husbands and partners. However, even though it's estimated that one in four couples in the UK sleep apart, this can be a very sensitive issue. 'I would hate for anyone to conclude that there was something wrong with our marriage if they knew we slept in separate rooms,' said one interviewee, even though she and her partner were at the time constantly disturbed by her hot sweats. Another interviewee said that her husband thought she was rejecting him when she said she wanted to sleep alone. 'Of course I'm not rejecting him, but I hate him near me when I'm so hot and bothered.'

However, one interviewee who was sleeping down the hallway from her husband found it rather titillating. 'We've got to the stage where it's better for us both to sleep separately, but I rather like the corridor-creeping that goes on when we're in the mood. It's like being teenagers again.'

So, although some couples clearly make the most of their new sleeping arrangements, for some women, the wish to sleep alone is a much more difficult issue to broach.

I asked interviewees who slept apart from their husbands and partners how best to tackle the subject. Being honest seemed the best policy, and reassuring their partner that needing space wasn't a personal rejection. That's fine if your partner understands, but as we've already found in this exploration of the realities of the menopause, communication can become very strained, or can even break down altogether.

Seeking emotional support

If you are experiencing communication difficulties, and want to try professional help, as I have already mentioned, your GP's surgery may be able to offer you counselling sessions. You may also have a local counselling centre in your area. Alternatively, you can find registered psychotherapists and counsellors in your region through the BACP (British Association for Counselling and Psychotherapy) or the UKCP (United Kingdom Council for Psychotherapy). See helpful websites at the end of the book.

The organization Relate describes itself as dedicated to the promotion of health, respect and justice in couple and family relationships. They have centres all over the country. The British Association for Sexual and Relationship Therapy (BASRT) is a national charity for sexual and relationship therapy, and has developed the Sensate Focus Programme, which has helped many couples with intimacy issues.

If you feel that going to a professional counsellor is not for you, here are a few golden rules of good listening which can help open up communication between you, whether or not menopause is somewhere in the equation.

Basic listening skills

Give yourselves time. These are important issues. Turn off the television, mobile phones or anything else that is a distraction. If necessary, book a date with each other that is specifically for this conversation.

Choose somewhere you both feel comfortable. For instance, it may be better not to have the conversation at home. Instead, try going for a walk together, or a cycle ride or find a private corner in a café or restaurant.

Be careful with alcohol. Alcohol can loosen tongues, but it can also create further conflict.

Be respectful. You each have your own experience of what's happening. Try and put other issues aside so you can listen to what your partner is saying and feeling, without interrupting them.

Be honest. It takes courage to admit that you might be feeling fear, guilt or rejection. But *don't* blame your partner for this. Blame shuts down communication.

Take turns to speak, and don't interrupt. Summarize back what you've heard – and park your own response until you're both agreed that each one of you has been correctly heard.

Show you are listening. Be attentive – look your partner in the eye. If it's getting fraught, agree to take a break and then come back again when you've both cooled off.

You may feel embarrassed or ashamed to talk about sex. This may be the first time you will ever have had a conversation like this. Some couples never talk about sex. Others may only allude to it. If you value your relationship, it's worth the risk, and you may be amazed at what you find out about each other.

Be aware of each other's past. One or both partners may have experienced some kind of abuse or neglect in childhood. This can have a drastic effect on how a child develops and is able to relate to other people as an adult. Many people never talk about what's happened to them and, with age, those childhood secrets can become increasingly toxic. Sexual changes during the menopause can bring old issues into the open. This can be a good opportunity to confront and deal with things that sometimes have been waiting decades for resolution.

Don't feel you have to fill silences. Silence can be the space where the greatest insights are gained. So don't push your partner or yourself if either of you need time to reflect on what you want to say or how you are feeling.

You can't fix each other. The mere act of naming difficult issues with a partner who is willing to listen can be hugely releasing and healing in itself, and can open a door to honest communication about how you might improve your relationship.

Get help. If it becomes too difficult, again, do consider talking with a professional counsellor.

Keeping fit

While it's essential to talk, it's also vital that you keep yourself fit and healthy. In researching this book, I was shocked to learn that 80 per cent of women in the UK do no exercise at all. Exercise is essential for everyone, but especially so for older women. It helps to build up bone density, strengthen muscle tone, generally control weight and generate a healthy balance of feel-good and stress-managing hormones in the system such as serotonin and endorphins, and adrenaline and cortisol. Experts say you need to do something to raise your heart rate at least three times a week, each time for around 30 minutes. This doesn't mean going on a ten-mile hike, taking part in triathlons, joining netball teams – or indeed tandeming across northern Spain – but it *does* mean making an effort of some kind.

Do find something that you enjoy, rather than what you think you 'ought' to be doing. Bashing away on machines at the gym is fine for some, but personally, I keep fit through a mixture of exercise including belly- and now tap-dancing, yoga, Pilates and once a week a bit of slow (as in totter) jogging. This combination increases my flexibility as well as my stamina, and I enjoy the class atmosphere. Hobbies such as regular gardening or walking the dog can also provide good exercise. Whatever you choose to do, have FUN, and promise yourself you'll keep it up.

Janice is a vibrant 61-year-old. She's an ex-dancer, and runs the Pilates and keep-fit classes I attend. She's very aware how few menopausal women realize the importance of exercise as part of managing the menopause, and is particularly keen on Pilates for women as a way of restoring and strengthening the body's natural balance. Pilates, she said, also gives you a sense of pride.

> It helps to ease aches and pains, but more importantly it increases flexibility. I know a lot of women who get frightened of falling as they get older. This means their lives grow smaller and smaller. Going regularly to Pilates helps them to overcome their fear. I always include balancing poses to raise their confidence. They can see how they improve each week, and how their core strength improves. Doing regular exercise makes you look better and feel better about yourself.

Exercise can help stress incontinence

Some of the women I interviewed mentioned in passing that they had developed stress incontinence (leaking urine when they laugh, cough, sneeze or sometimes just walk). This embarrassing and distressing condition is caused mainly by weakened pelvic floor muscles following childbirth. Loss of muscle tone increases as we go through the menopause.

Simone, who runs the gym where my Pilates classes are held, told me of an exercise programme that had helped her.

> I had huge pelvic floor problems, to the extent that I had no bladder control at all. The cause of this was partly my psychological makeup – I was very obese as a child, and had a difficult birth with one of my children. And then there was the ageing process on top.
>
> My doctors wanted me to have radical surgery, which meant giving up my career as a health instructor. I refused, and did everything I could naturally. I did lots of pelvic floor contractions to strengthen my muscles as well as my core. It worked. I used to wear pads all the time, now I don't need them. It was hard work, but very worthwhile. If you've got a problem like this, my advice is to start doing pelvic floor exercises now!
>
> Our bodies change when we go through the menopause. Exercise helps to balance our hormones. We also need to drink more fluids. But a lot of women aren't too keen to do this because they are scared they will lose control of their bladder. What I would say to them is, with a bit of effort you can get back in control of this.

Simone has developed an exercise guide to strengthen pelvic floor muscles. Simone's Gym contact details are at the end of the book under women's general health.

Yoga

I have been practising yoga for many years. I have always found it helpful for my general welfare, especially now I am older. Judi Sweeting, a senior Iyengar yoga teacher who co-runs the Cotswold Iyengar Yoga Centre, believes yoga is very beneficial for women of all ages, and can be particularly helpful to those approaching the early stages of menopause.

A lot of women don't realize the symptoms they are having indicate it's menopause time. Yoga helps them to connect with their bodies and listen to what's going on. In addition, yoga calms you down and helps you to balance your mind, body and spirit. It's especially good for managing panic attacks. I experienced this myself during the onset of menopause. I found them very distressing at the time, because I kept on thinking something dreadful was about to happen. Practising yoga helped me to find a sense of calmness in amongst the confusion.

Judi also believes yoga is an excellent way to control many specific symptoms of the menopause as well as other medical conditions that can arise.

If a woman is having hot flushes she can learn to do cooling poses, such as forward bends. Other poses like twists and inversions tend to heat up the body, so it's a question of understanding what works for you at any given time.

Different poses can also help to release anger that a lot of women experience during the menopause, as well as managing inappropriate surges of sexual desire.

It's very beneficial for women who have cancer, too. By teaching them recuperative poses, they can learn to keep the cancerous cells quiet. You can also use yoga for medical conditions such as vaginal and rectal prolapses. These can be reversed if you catch them in time. Upside-down poses pull up the internal muscles, and yoga is great for preventing fibroids from getting too hard.

There are poses to soften the stomach area, which you can do until the fibroids naturally shrink during the menopause. Yoga can even help endometriosis as well as increasing overall flexibility – and being able to stand on your head at the age of 60 is a great confidence booster.

I asked Judi what advice she would give to a younger woman heading for the menopause.

At the end of the day, it's down to you to grab the reins of your unruly mind, and turn negative thinking into positive thought. Yoga is brilliant for that. It's just a very practical way to keep healthy.

Dancing

If you hate going to the gym or the thought of a disciplined yoga practice, you might consider taking up something fun like dance. We have already heard in Chapter 4 how Biodanza rejuvenated 69-year-old Barbara.

Wendy Buonaventura, author of *I Put A Spell On You* (about women and dance) and director of the annual Sirocco Dance Festival, believes that dance is a marvellous way to keep fit as you get older. Wendy looks on all forms of dance as a learning experience, in the sense that they connect you to your spirit. 'It helps to let out those locked-up emotions and express what you really feel,' she told me. Her life motto is, 'Use it or lose it'.

> In traditional tribal rituals, group dances are used to drive away evil demons. For us in our Western culture, it's about using dance to get away from our sedentary lives. It's too easy to get locked onto the computer or sit around watching television. These days we have become consumers of other people's entertainment. Not so long ago we used to entertain ourselves, sing around the piano, or go out to dance socially. That was how we kept our energy moving and our enjoyment of life. It's a shame it's gone.

For women who are keen to take up dance later in their lives, Wendy says it's important to find a dance style that suits you, and to give yourself time to start enjoying it.

> Older women are often drawn to Arabic dance or tap-dancing because it's such fun, and you can do it on your own. Couple dancing is different. For a start, you need a partner, and that can be quite daunting for some women if they don't have husbands or partners willing to go with them. So these types of dances can be fraught with the potential to feel bad about yourself. When I started learning the tango I used to get depressed because I felt no-one wanted to dance with me.
>
> But once I stopped caring, I felt much better and started to enjoy myself whether I was dancing or sitting out having a chat. Now, I notice that young men are very happy to dance with an older woman as long as she can dance well. Age doesn't matter at all.

As Wendy mentioned, Arabic dancing (more commonly called belly-dancing) is one of the most popular forms of dance for older women.

Hazel Kayes has been teaching it for years and is passionate about the benefits for menopausal and postmenopausal women.

> Bellydancing helps because the movements work from inside, right through to your spine and deep into your pelvis. It builds up muscle tone to protect the bones as well as massaging your internal organs. It also keeps you supple, in shape, and stops your hips from stiffening up. In addition, it helps to prevent osteoporosis, rheumatism and arthritis.
>
> We don't do a lot of feminine things in our society these days, so having the opportunity to dress up in all that sparkly stuff is terrific, apart from being sexy. It's a chance to feel connected with yourself as a woman, and there's no age limit to that.
>
> The oldest woman I have taught was 70. She's now teaching bellydancing herself. I also taught a grandmother, mother and daughter at the same time. They were great fun. The grandmother took off with a man she met on the internet, and is now living in the Middle East. Just goes to show you can't plan life, and you have no control over what happens!

Older relationships, it seems, can certainly be life changing! Deidre, a participant I met at the Sirocco Festival, comes every year just to have a good time dancing with other women. She told me,

> I didn't start bellydancing until I was 49. I love the movement and freedom – to be able to move through space and express myself. It gives me such joy to use my arms and legs in this way. Not everyone is so lucky.
>
> I never had a chance to dance when I was younger. I had too much to do bringing up children. Now they have left home I can please myself. Dancing helps me to relax, and to connect with myself and the world around me. It's taught me to love the sensation of my body moving, even when I'm just walking. I would say to any older woman, start doing it! Yes, it does take longer to learn movements and to become flexible. But the benefits to your health are fantastic. It gives you core strength, helps to maintain your weight and is excellent for general well-being.

There are many other ways to enjoy keeping fit and healthy. The most important thing is not to use the menopause as an excuse to give up on yourself. These days you could have at least a third of your life left to live, and you need a healthy body and a healthy mind to get the best out of it.

Whatever you choose to do naturally for yourself, I highly recommend Marilyn Glenville's *Natural Alternatives to HRT*. It provides clear, sensible advice and information on a whole range of issues to do with health and the menopause.

This brings the exploration of our M-words to a close. It's time to it wrap it up with a final message to Meg, whose question at the very beginning about the difference between being fertile and coming to the end of childbearing years lies at the heart of this book.

Message to Meg

Dear Meg

I realize you probably don't want to think about the future at the moment. Recovering from a difficult divorce and getting used to being the single mum of three children approaching teen years is enough for anyone to cope with. But I hope this book will have helped you understand that the menopause, when it happens to you – which it will – will be a much bigger and richer experience than you can currently imagine.

I also want to tell you how sad I am that (regrettably, like so many of us) when you were young, your mother never spoke to you about your femininity and sexuality. I can imagine how alarming it must have felt to be handed that box of sanitary pads when you were sent to boarding school, with no idea what they were for. I also suspect that when your periods started, no-one paid much attention to your entry into womanhood. My guess is that it became your monthly 'curse'.

When we are brought up to see the very essence of our femininity as an unpleasant bodily function, it's hard to adjust to the wonderful natural cycles of *being* a woman. But, Meg, the menopause is not a dysfunction or a disease. Neither can it be limited to a medical classification which says you're through it once you've stopped menstruating for 12 months. Be prepared for it to take years for you to adjust to this completely different stage in life, one where, as we learnt from that older female gorilla, you are at the mercy of your changing hormones.

I understand that, right now, this might be hard to take in. As you said when we spoke, and rightly so for any woman of your age, sexuality is central to who you are. In my early 40s, I couldn't have believed that one day I would lose interest in sex. All I can tell you is that what happens to your libido during the menopause is very different from being, as you said, in a 'dreadful relationship'.

These sexual changes are a natural response to falling hormone levels, and, anyway, you may be one of those women for whom sex continues to be fun and, on the whole, problem-free. On the other hand, your sexual desire may also drop overnight. Or you may find sex so painful that you don't want it at all. But as we've also heard from the men who spoke in this book, it certainly doesn't have to mean the end of a relationship. I hope you might remember that as long as you can talk honestly with your partner, you can find other ways to enjoy intimacy and sensuality.

Of course, this shift in sexuality coincides with other midlife stresses too, especially as you move away from active motherhood. And, that's really what I've wanted to convey to you. The menopause will be for you the time when you step across the threshold into your third age, and reassess what really matters as you.

I was, however, heartened to learn when we spoke that you're good at accepting things. This will help you to embrace whatever happens to you as an opportunity to deepen your understanding of who you are. It will also make it easier for you to go through the menopause as naturally as possible.

Then again, you may decide that you want to manage your ageing process actively, and perhaps use hormone replacement treatments. Just remember that while HRT has its place in helping some women through a critical period, there comes a time when we are no longer able to impose our will on nature. Even women taking HRT still age. It's what our bodies do.

Whatever choice you make, it's important to know you will not be the same woman as you are today. That's the physical reality. But, as we've heard from so many vibrant, perceptive, jubilant, and different postmenopausal women in this book, neither does this mean the end of the road.

Yes, you will watch your daughter blossom, and you may mourn your youth and the loss of your fertility. But if you can learn to listen to the shifts that are happening inside, you will become aware of an older, wiser self waiting for you as you come to terms with it all. That's when you can look in the mirror, square your shoulders and get on with life the way *you* want to live it.

So, Meg, I hope this book has given you – using your own words when we spoke – the clear, non-hysterical information you asked for. Certainly, the menopause *will* be the end of womanhood as you know it today. But, if you can see this transition as a sacred rite of passage rather than as a dysfunction, you will be able to draw on all the heartbreaks and joys, disappointments and triumphs that women have been through since time began, and put this wisdom to good use.

Women who have gone through the menopause can be inspirational, astute, deliciously eccentric and full of fun. To my mind, it's the greatest sisterhood in the world.

Recommended reading

Bair, Deirdre. *Calling It Quits: Late-Life Divorce and Starting Over*. Random House, New York, 2007.

Baron, Renee & Wagele, Elizabeth. *The Enneagram Made Easy: Discover the 9 Types of People*. Harper Thorsons, San Francisco, 1994.

Bowie, Fiona (comp.). *The Wisdom of Hildegard of Bingen*. Lion Publishing, Oxford, UK, 1997.

Brings, Felicia & Winter, Susan. *Older Women, Younger Men*. New Horizon Press, Far Hills, NJ, 2000.

Buonaventura, Wendy. *Serpent in the Nile*. 2nd edn, Saqi Books, London, 2010.

Coughlin, Lin, Wingard, Ellen & Hollihan, Keith (eds). *Enlightened Power: How Women are Transforming the Practice of Leadership*. Jossey-Bass, San Francisco, 2005.

D'Adamo, Dr Peter. *Eat Right For Your Blood Type*. Putman, New York, 1996.

Dawkins, Richard. *The Selfish Gene*. Oxford University Press, Oxford, UK, 2006.

Foxcroft, Louise. *Hot Flushes, Cold Science*. Granta Publications, London, 2009.

Frankl, Viktor. *Man's Search for Meaning*. Pocket Books, New York, 1959.

Gateley, Edwina. *Soul Sisters: Women in Scripture Speak to Women of Today*. Orbis Books, New York, 2007.

Gilbert, Elizabeth. *Eat, Pray, Love*. Bloomsbury, London, 2006.

Glenville, Marilyn. *Natural Alternatives to HRT*. Kylie Cathie Ltd, London, 1997.

Greer, Germaine. *The Change*. Ballantine Books, New York, 1993.

Handy, Charles and Handy, Elizabeth. *Reinvented Lives. Women at Sixty: A Celebration*. Hutchinson, London, 2007.

Harvey, John H., Wenzel, Amy & Sprecher, Susan (eds). *The Handbook of Sexuality in Close Relationships*. Lawrence Erlbaum Associates, New York, 2004.

Horrigan, Bonnie. *Red Moon Passage*. Harper Thorsons, San Francisco, 1996.

Houck, Judith. *Hot and Bothered: Women, Medicine, and the Menopause*. Harvard University Press, Cambridge, MA, 2008.

Ironside, Virginia. *The Virginia Monologues: Why Growing Old is Great*. Fig Tree, London, 2009.

Jung, Carl. *Memories, Dreams and Reflections*. Vintage Books, New York, 1989.

Kaschak, Ellyn & Tiefer, Leonore. *A New View of Women's Sexual Problems*. Routledge, Abingdon, UK, 2002.

Lee, John, with Hopkins, Virginia. *What Your Doctor May Not Tell You About Menopause: The Breakthrough Book on Natural Progesterone*. Grand Central Publishing, New York, 1996.

Loe, Meika. *The Rise of Viagra: How the Little Blue Pill Changed Sex in America*. New York University Press, New York, 2005.

Maltz, Wendy. *The Porn Trap: The Essential Guide to Overcoming Problems Caused by Pornography*. Harper Paperbacks, New York, 2009.

Maltz, Wendy. *The Sexual Healing Journey: A Guide for Survivors of Sexual Abuse*. Harper Paperbacks, New York, 2001.

Mann, A. T. *The Round Art of Astrology*. Vega, London, 2003.

McCarthy, Barry & McCarthy, Emily. *Discovering Your Couple Sexual Style*. Routledge, New York, 2009.

Moody, Harry R. & Carroll, David. *The Five Stages of the Soul: Charting the Spiritual Passages that Shape our Lives*. Rider, London, 1997.

Moore, Thomas. *Dark Nights of the Soul*. Gotham, New York, 2005.

Morgentaler, Abraham. *The Viagra Myth: The Surprising Impact on Love and Relationships*. Jossey-Bass, San Francisco, 2003.

Moynihan, Ray & Mintzes, Barbara. *Sex, Lies and Pharmaceuticals: How Drug Companies Plan to Profit from Female Sexual Dysfunction*. Greystone Books, Vancouver, Canada, 2010.

Northrup, Christiane. *The Secret Pleasures of the Menopause*. Hay House, Sydney, Australia, 2008.

Owen, Lara. *Her Blood Is Gold: Celebrating the Power of Menstruation*. Harper Collins, San Francisco, 1993.

Pope, Alexandra & Bennett, Jane. *The Pill: Are You Sure It's for You?* Allen & Unwin, Sydney, Australia, 2009.

Rako, Dr Susan. *The Hormone of Desire: The Truth about Sexuality, Menopause, and Testosterone*. Three Rivers Press, New York, 1996.

Robinson, Dr Helen. 'A beginner's guide to tantric sex', *Psychologies*, January 2008, pp. 55–8.

Rountree, Cathleen. *On Women Turning Fifty*. Harper, San Francisco, 1993.

Ruddock, Jill Shaw. *The Second Half of Your Life*. Random House, New York, publishing date: March 2011.

Shapiro Barash, Susan. *A Passion for More*. Berkeley Hills Books, Albany, CA, 2001.

Sheehy, Gail. *The Silent Passage: Menopause*. Random House, New York, 1991.

Shuttle, Penelope & Redgrove, Peter. *The Wise Wound, Menstruation and Everywoman*. Paladin Grafton Books, London, 1978.

Smith, Myrrha Stanford. *The Great Lie*. HONNO Welsh Women's Press, Aberystwyth, Wales, 2010.

Sparrowe, Linda & Walden, Patricia. *The Woman's Book of Yoga and Health*. Shambhala, Boston and London, 2002.

Stoppard, Dr Miriam. *Menopause*. Dorling Kindersley, London, 1994.

Trimberger, E. Kay. *The New Single Woman*. Beacon Press, Boston, 2005.

Webber, Christine. *Too Young to Get Old: The Baby Boomer's Guide to Living Life in the Full*. Piatkus, London, 2010.

Williamson, Marianne. *A Return to Love*. The Aquarian Press, Wellingborough, England, 1992.

Wilson, Robert. *Feminine Forever*. W. H. Allen, London, 1996.

Wingert, Pat & Kantrowitz, Barbara. *The Menopause Book*. Workman Publishing Company, New York, 2009.

Wyatt, Gail & Wyatt Jr., Lewis. *No More Clueless Sex*. John Wiley & Sons, Hoboken, NJ, 2003.

Helpful websites

(Most have links to other good websites.)

Aging
Center for Aging, Sexuality, and Meaning (based in USA)
www.casam.info

Bladder and bowel incontinence
Bladder and Bowel Foundation
www.bladderandbowelfoundation.org

Cancer care
Cancer Research UK
www.cancerresearchuk.org
Breast cancer
www.cancerfightingstrategies.com
Breast cancer care
www.breastcancercare.org.uk
Prostate cancer
www.prostate-cancer.org.uk

Counselling and psychotherapy
BACP (British Association for Counsellors and Psychotherapists)
General enquiries: 01455883300
www.bacp.co.uk
UKCP (United Kingdom Council for Psychotherapists)
General enquiries: 02070149955
www.psychotherapy.org.uk
Relate
www.relate.org.uk

Dance
Biodanza
www.biodanzascotland.com

Sirocco Dance Festival
www.siroccofestival.org.uk

Dating websites
Friends over Fifty
www.friendsoverfifty.co.uk
Friends Reunited
www.friendsreunited.com
Go Cougar
www.GoCougar.com
Toyboyflirt
www.toyboyflirt.co.uk

Education
University of the Third Age
www.u3a.org.uk

Herbalists
National Institute of Medical Herbalists
www.nimh.org.uk

Homeopathy
ABC of Homeopathy
www.abchomeopathy.com
Neal's Yard Remedies
www.nealsyardremedies.com

Hysterectomy information and support
The Hysterectomy Association
Telephone: 08717811141
Email: info@hysterectomy-association. org.uk
Website: www.hysterectomy-association.org.uk

HRT and localized HRT:

Bioidentical Hormone Replacement Therapy (BHRT)
www.medicalnewstoday.com
Flibanserin
www.flibanserininformation.com
Intrinsa
www.netdoctor.co.uk
National Heart, Lung, and Blood Institute
www.nhlbi.nih.gov (put HRT in search)
Vagifem (localized)
www.xpil.medicines.org.uk

Menopause websites

BBC on menopause
www.bbc.co.uk/health
International Menopause Society
www.imsociety.org
Medic8
www.medic8.com
Menopause Exchange
www.menopause-exchange.co.uk
Menopause Matters (includes comprehensive list of menopause books)
www.menopausematters.co.uk
Menopause Support
www.menopausesupport.org.uk
New View Campaign
www.newviewcampaign.org
Power Surge book list
www.power-surge.com

Menstruation

Alexandra Pope
www.wildgenie.com

National UK menopause clinics

www.menopauseclinics.org

Personal development

The Hoffman Process
When you are serious about change

Tel: 01903 88 99 90
Email: info@hoffmaninstitute.co.uk
www.hoffmaninstitute.co.uk

Sex (general)

Channel 4: The Sex Show
www.sexperienceuk.channel4.com
Sexual Advice Association
www.sda.uk.net

Sex shop (for women)

Sh!
www.sh-womenstore.com

Sex therapy

British Association for Sexual and Relationship Therapy
www.BASRT.org.uk
Human Awareness Institute
www.hai.org
Sensate Focus Programme
www.basmt.org.uk
Tantric workshops
www.loveforcouples.com

Women's general health

Savvy Woman
www.savvywoman.co.uk
Simone's Gyms
www.simones.co.uk
Real Women
www.wearerealwomen.wordpress.com
Women's Resource Centre
www.wrc.org.uk
Women Speak
www.womenspeak.com
Women's Sport and Fitness Foundation
www.wsff.org.uk

Volunteer organizations

Voluntary Services Overseas
www.vso.org.uk

Yoga

Cotswold Iyengar Yoga Centre
www.cotswoldiyengar.co.uk

Index

affair 72, 112, 114, 117, 119, 122

ageing process 2, 5–6, 14, 19–20, 26, 28, 72–3, 89, 95–6, 98, 110–13, 118, 122, 133–4, 140, 150

alcohol 101, 144–5, 148

Allen, Paula Gunn 85

anger 3, 91, 124

anxiety 12, 36–7, 81, 112, 130, 134, 144–5

arthritis 132, 134, 137, 153

attitudes 2, 5, 17–18, 115, 117

women's 20

Augustine of Hippo 92

Bisset, Jacqueline 16

body image 79, 122

Bolen, Jean Shinoda 85

bonds with others 81, 93, 119, 121

bone density 149

bones, protecting 142, 153

Born, Caroline 97

Botox 16, 136

brain 26, 29, 71, 114–15, 134, 140–1

breast cancer 56, 88–9, 115, 133–4 see also cancer

Brice-Ytsma, Hanaja 135, 140

Buonaventura, Wendy 152, 157

Buscaglia, Leo 86

caffeine 145

cancer 35, 127, 135, 143, 151 see also breast cancer

careers 9, 29, 36, 150

CBT (cognitive behavioural therapy) 145

celibacy 76, 93, 95

change
hormonal 44, 112, 143
identity 1
life 1, 88, 101, 131
physical 7, 13, 21, 79–80, 142
psychological 6, 21, 66
sexual 5, 12–13, 21, 43, 49, 51, 55, 64, 66, 78, 95, 106, 111
spiritual 2

children 9, 12, 22–3, 31–3, 35, 38, 40, 49–50, 52, 65, 71–3, 88–9, 108–10, 117–18, 120–2, 153–4

Colas, Kathryn 38, 129

Collins, Jackie 116

communication 3, 27, 44, 52, 61, 72, 94, 106, 110, 125, 147–8

community 17, 19, 81

condoms 45, 75, 78

confidence 107, 129, 138, 149
loss of 37

confusion 3, 87, 92, 151

constipation 143

control 21, 26, 30, 40, 62, 76, 78, 99, 120, 138, 145, 150–1, 153

counselling 72, 74, 78, 130–2, 147

Crammer, Liz 15

creativity 12, 81, 105
crises 7–8, 12–13, 43, 72, 80–2
crone 85–6
cultures 17–19, 24, 110, 119, 122

dance 152–3
daughter 18, 26–9, 32, 36, 89–90, 107–8, 153
death 3, 21–3, 48, 55–6, 77, 83–4, 87, 89–90
Dennerstein, Lorraine 17, 46, 51, 134
depression 14, 35, 51, 79, 138, 152
despair 16, 25, 66, 82, 104–5
distress 6, 38, 50, 56, 95, 99, 128, 145–6
divorce 22, 30, 33, 35, 45, 49, 74, 76–8, 88, 109–10, 114–15
rate 74, 78
doctors 62, 114, 118, 141, 150 see also GPs
and diagnosis 12, 32
and drugs 15
and embarrassment 58
experiences of talking to 127–8, 130–3
female 131
and HRT 132–3, 136–7
dopamine 71
dreams 10, 32–3, 48, 100, 105, 122
drug companies 11, 15
drugs 12–15, 52, 71, 127
dryness 127, 139, 141, 144
dysfunction 5, 11–13, 43, 51, 154, 156

elder stateswomen 37, 96
emotional
intelligence 45, 84
support 147
emotions 88, 103, 112, 123, 152

empty nest syndrome 12–13
endorphins 121
energies 12, 23, 85, 91, 152
sexual 48–50
Erikson, Erik 81
exercise 7, 115, 141, 145, 149–50

failure 15, 56, 82
family 19, 32, 39, 62, 81, 83, 90–1, 100, 109, 122, 129
femininity 17, 65, 94, 96, 99, 125, 153–4
fertility 15, 22, 30, 45, 83, 155
fibroids 138, 151
forgetting see memory loss
Foxcroft, Louise 133
fun 2, 7, 11, 77, 93, 96, 121, 149, 152, 155–6

Gateley, Edwina 97
gay 5, 16, 100, 127
relationships 63, 100
Gilbert, Elizabeth 3
Glanzman, Louis 97
Glenville, Marilyn 12, 154
GPs 112–13, 127–8, 130–3, 137–8, 140 see also doctors
Green, Adele 19
Greer, Germaine 2, 25
grief 22, 31, 33, 81, 87, 106, 108, 115, 131, 145
guilt 3, 60, 63–4, 82, 89, 118, 125, 148
gym 23, 142, 149–50, 152
gynaecologist 130–1, 138–9

hair loss 13–14, 138
headaches 1, 143
health 10, 53, 76–7, 131, 140, 147, 150, 153–4
health professionals, alternative 10, 28, 134

herbal remedies 135, 143
herbalists 135, 140–1
HIV 74
hormone levels 7, 12, 143, 155
hormones 9, 14, 95, 135, 138,
150, 154
Horrigan, Bonnie 83–4
hot flushes 1, 12, 32, 38, 44, 108,
124–5, 132–3, 138, 140, 143, 145
Houck, Judith 133
HRT (hormone replacement
therapy) 2, 5–6, 11, 14, 27, 43,
48, 60–1, 65, 73, 76, 107, 127,
132–40
humour 41, 98, 105
husband 2–4, 7, 23–4, 31, 34–5,
49–50, 52–7, 59–73, 75–7, 88,
90, 101, 128–30, 136–7, 139–40,
146–7
hysterectomy 14, 101, 111, 132,
137–8

images 16, 26, 110–11, 122, 154
International Menopause Society
17
internet 34, 70–1, 75, 78, 111,
114–15, 142, 144, 153
intimacy 51, 56, 63–4, 67, 82, 93,
117, 125, 155
Ironside, Virginia 93
irrationality 113
isolation 10, 32, 82, 87

Jacobi, Jolande 82
Jannini, Emmanuele 15
journey 5, 83–4, 86, 97–8
Jung, Carl 82–3, 94

Kagawa, Noriko 20
Kayes, Hazel 153
Keller, Helen 82
Kenton, Lesley 21, 86

Kundalini energy 94
Kutenai, Kachinas 94

lesbian *see* gay
liberation 9, 28, 45, 87
libido 2–3, 11–12, 14, 17, 21, 48,
50–2, 56–8, 60–2, 64, 78, 89,
94–5, 98, 141–2
loss of 2, 11–12, 21, 44, 51, 56,
64, 78, 89, 98, 134
listening 147–9
Loe, Meika 13
love 25, 32–3, 35, 50, 52–4, 56–8,
65–7, 70, 86–7, 90–1, 100, 105,
113–16, 118–20
lovers 50, 57, 70, 77, 80, 83,
107–8, 118
lubricants 49, 58, 61, 70, 105,
116, 128–9
natural 144

Macpherson, Elle 16
male menopause 7, 114, 116–17,
119
Maltz, Wendy 47, 71, 79
marriage 5, 9, 47, 50, 63, 74, 77,
88, 90, 93, 95, 103, 105, 109–10,
116–17, 121–3
masturbation 67–71, 109, 112,
122, 125
maturing 86, 100, 112, 119, 121
media 15, 26, 37, 62, 67, 111,
123, 125
medical conditions 21, 129, 140,
151
memory loss 124, 141–2
menopausal
age 5, 141
symptoms 12, 14, 18, 130,
132–4, 140, 142
wives 4, 104
menopause clinics 131

menstruation 22, 43, 97, 124, 135
midlife
    crisis 8, 43, 72, 80–2
    and men 7–8, 83
    sexual activity in 47
    and spirituality 82
    transition 81
    and women 14, 83, 155
mood swings 7, 113, 117, 123,
    132, 138–9, 143
Moore, Thomas 83, 94
Morgentaler, Abraham 13
Mother Theresa 91
Moynihan, Ray 11
myths 9, 20–1, 41

natural
    alternatives to HRT 140
    progesterone 142
New Age 86, 96

oestrogen 26, 58, 132, 141–2
    levels 11, 48, 140, 142, 144
orgasm 12, 15, 53, 55, 66, 71, 94,
    105, 124
Osborne, Sharon 16
osteoporosis 130, 132, 134, 153
ovaries 7, 48, 78, 94, 111, 142

pains 10, 22, 24–5, 87, 117, 149
panic attacks 145, 151
partners 13–14, 30, 33–5, 50–1,
    54–6, 60–3, 65–6, 68–9, 71–2,
    75–6, 100, 103–6, 113, 116,
    124–5, 146–8
partnership 5, 104, 117
penetrative sex 48, 54, 57–61,
    116, 124, 139 see also sexual
    intercourse
periods 1, 3, 7, 21–2, 30–1, 52,
    120, 123–4, 137, 154
    irregular 109

personal
    choice 132–3
    growth 79, 88
perspective 5–6, 93–4, 97, 99
pessaries 59, 128, 133, 139
pills, contraceptive 135
Pope, Alexandra 79, 84, 135
pornography 70–2, 75, 104,
    113–14, 116, 122, 125
postmenopausal
    sex 91
    women 43, 76, 80, 87, 101,
        107, 118, 122, 153, 155
power 21, 31, 80, 86–7, 94, 135
progesterone 48, 142
progesterone cream, natural 3,
    142
prostitution 41, 69, 75–6, 114,
    125

Rako, Susan 14
rape 60, 123
regeneration 18–19
Reich, William 94
rejection 67, 124, 148
Relate 74
relationships 5, 13, 35, 43–4,
    47–8, 51, 53–8, 62–6, 72–5,
    77–8, 104, 107–9, 111, 115–17,
    121–4, 148
    open 104
relief 25, 28–9, 31, 61, 70, 88,
    105, 120
religion 115
renewal 18–19, 36
rite of passage 95–6, 156
rituals 95–7
roles 10, 17, 28, 62, 83, 90, 93,
    118–20

sacred state 85
self-esteem 12, 51, 81, 130

self interest 123

sensuality 93–4, 99, 124–5, 155

sex

  masturbatory 114

  oral 47–8

  painful 2, 44, 58–9, 132, 139, 141

  postmenopausal 91

  tantric 93, 158

sex drive 49–50, 53, 56, 61, 63, 134, 142

sex life 34, 44, 50, 55–6, 61, 65, 69–70, 100, 104–5, 116, 123–4, 127, 139–40

sex toys 68–70, 128–9

sex workers 41, 75–6

sexual intercourse 47, 67–8, 93 *see also* penetrative sex

sexual relationship 49, 52, 60, 70, 113, 115

sexuality 1, 11, 14, 20, 25, 47, 65, 79, 94, 96, 124, 133, 154–5

sexually transmitted diseases (STDs) 74, 78

shame 82, 116, 124–5, 152

Sheehy, Gail 133

sin 91–3

sleep 52, 62–3, 70, 138, 146–7

Sophocles 94

spirituality 11, 79–81, 86, 91, 94, 108, 118, 123

Stanford-Smith, Myrrha 101

STDs (sexually transmitted diseases) 74, 78

stress 48, 65–6, 144–5, 149

  incontinence 15, 150

struggle 22, 25, 43, 76, 83, 92, 96, 115, 141

surge 48, 71, 151

surrender 87

sweats 111, 113, 146

Sweeting, Judi 150

SWOFTIES 76–7

symptoms 7, 12, 18, 22, 66, 111–12, 130, 132, 136–8, 140, 142, 145, 151

taboos 3, 5–6, 19, 44, 67, 69, 117, 120, 122

testosterone 14, 48, 71, 77

tests 131

therapy 67, 75, 80, 87

  alternative 135

Thoreau 104, 110

transition 1, 5–6, 12, 20–1, 28–9, 82, 85, 95, 110, 138, 156

  spiritual 84

treatment 5–6, 13, 51–2, 56, 130, 133–4

trust 12, 52, 81–2, 99, 101, 126

truth 14, 54, 64, 82, 97–8, 105, 107

vagina 133, 139, 141, 144

vaginal

  atrophy 2, 58, 125, 130, 141, 144

  dryness 12, 58, 66, 116, 128, 139, 144

  orgasm 15, 116

Viagra 13, 125

weight gain 13–14, 16, 24, 38 139, 142

Weintraub, Arlene 14

Western societies 6, 9, 18–19, 91, 119

wig 138

Williamson, Marianne 87

Wilson, Robert 133

Winterich, Julie 13, 16, 66

wisdom 10–11, 86, 97–8, 104, 120–1, 125, 156

woman's body 12, 58, 124
women
　older 5–6, 9–11, 14–15,
　　17–18, 21–2, 24–6, 33,
　　36–8, 41, 45, 49, 62,
　　71, 76–9, 83, 97–8, 100,

　　108, 111–12, 121–2,
　　128, 152
　working 36, 38, 40
workplace 36, 122

yoga 110, 149–51